Ancient Peoples and Places

THE ARMENIANS

General Editor

DR. GLYN DANIEL

ABOUT THE AUTHOR

Sirarpie Der Nersessian is a French citizen but Armenian by birth. She studied history and art history at the Sorbonne, from which she received her degree of Docteur ès Lettres in 1936. From 1926 to 1929 she was Chargée de Conférences in the Ecole Pratique des Hautes Etudes in Paris. In 1930 she went to Wellesley College, Wellesley, Mass., first as Lecturer, then as Professor of Art and, from 1937 to 1946, Chairman of the Department of Art and Director of the Farnsworth Museum. In 1946 she was appointed Professor of Byzantine Art and Archaeology at Dumbarton Oaks, and Member of the Faculty of Arts and Sciences at Harvard University, becoming Professor Emerita in 1963. Professor Der Nersessian has lectured at various universities in the United States and France, and has won academic distinction in both countries. She is a Fellow of the Mediaeval Academy of America, Associate Member of the Société Nationale des Antiquaires de France, and Member of the Academy of Sciences of Erevan, Armenia.

THE
ARMENIANS

Sirarpie Der Nersessian

78 PHOTOGRAPHS
48 LINE DRAWINGS
2 MAPS

PRAEGER PUBLISHERS
New York · Washington

THIS IS VOLUME SIXTY-EIGHT IN THE SERIES
Ancient Peoples and Places
GENERAL EDITOR: DR. GLYN DANIEL

BOOKS THAT MATTER

Published in the United States of America in 1970
by Praeger Publishers, Inc.
111 Fourth Avenue, New York, N.Y. 10003
© 1969 in London, England, by Sirarpie Der Nersessian
All rights reserved
Library of Congress Catalog Card Number: 78–92586
Printed in Great Britain

CONTENTS

ILLUSTRATIONS

9

The Land and its Early Inhabitants

Fig. 1

ARMENIA is the tableland which lies roughly between 37°
and 49° longitude East, and 37.5° and 41.5° latitude
North, and covers an area of approximately 300,000 sq. km.
This plateau, which forms part of a continuous system extending
from Asia Minor to Iran, dominates the neighbouring areas, its
altitude ranging from 800 close to 2000 m. It is buttressed on the
north by the Pontic Range and on the south by the Taurus,
which constitute formidable barriers. Between these limits,
several chains of mountains cross the country, following a
general easterly and south-easterly direction, and they separate
the land into a number of distinct sections with difficult passages
from north to south. Lofty peaks of volcanic origin rise high up
above the plateau. The principal ones are: the majestic cone of
Great Ararat (5205 m.), with next to it the Little Ararat
(3914 m.) in the heart of the country; the Alagöz (Aragats,
4180 m.) to the North of Mount Ararat and the Tendurek
(3548 m.) to the south. To the west rises the Bingöl dagh
(3650 m.), the 'mountain of a thousand tarns', from which
spring the Arax river and the principal tributaries of the
Euphrates. Mount Sipan (4176 m.) is north of Lake Van and
the massive formation of Nimrud dagh (2910 m.), with a lake
in its immense crater, rises to the west of the same lake. Many
of the rivers are mountain torrents running in deep gorges
between towering cliffs; the longest of these, the Arax, threading
through the plain of Ararat, proceeds southward and then
north-east to join the Kura and flow into the Caspian sea. In
the plain of Ararat, the largest and most fertile of the plains,
were founded the ancient cities of Armenia. The Lake of Van,
which covers an area of 3733 sq. km., is an inland sea, at an
altitude of 1590 m.; its waters are heavily charged with soda.

Plate 1

To the north-east, the alpine Lake of Sevan, surrounded by a circle of mountains, has an elevation of 1916 m. and an area of 1416 sq. km. The Lake of Urmia on the south east lies outside the limits of historical Armenia though forming part of the geographical complex.

The winters are long and very severe; in the high plateaux the snow can lie for up to eight months, but during the short and very hot summers the whole country bursts into life. Thanks to this brief interlude and to the natural fertility of the arable soil, where the decomposition of volcanic elements, mingled with the sediments of the Miocene and Pliocene, have constituted 'black earths', cereals are cultivated and there are rich pastures for the cattle. The valley of the Arax and the surroundings of Lake Van have vineyards and orchards, and on the sheltered north shore of this lake even olive trees can grow.

The subsoil is rich in ores of all kinds: the minerals include gold, silver, copper and iron, and there are important salt mines; borax and arsenic are abundant in the region of Lake Van. Because of the volcanic formation of the land there are large supplies of obsidian, and the tufa stone is well suited for building purposes. The 'kermes', an aphis found in the spring on the roots of a plant growing on the slopes of Mount Ararat, is a valuable asset, being the source of the highly appreciated red substance used for dyeing woollen and silk fabrics.

The Armenian highland which forms a natural bastion dominating the neighbouring lands, is less well protected by natural barriers on its eastern and western borders. It is in this general direction that the invasion routes lay and the main trade routes ran; hence this conformation of the land explains many aspects of Armenia's history.

Systematic explorations of numerous sites on the slopes of Mount Aragats and Mount Ararat, at Satani-dar and along the middle course of the river Hrazdan have shown that the Armenian highlands have been inhabited ever since the Lower

Fig. 1 Armenia and neighbouring lands

Palaeolithic period. The stone implements found in the succes/
sive layers of these areas display the characteristic features of the
artifacts of that period, and the improved techniques of the
Middle and Upper Palaeolithic ages. The hunting scenes
carved on the surfaces of cliffs and rocks by the cave/dwellers
of the Middle Stone age represent men armed with bow and
arrows, and accompanied by dogs, who pursue reindeer,
chamois and wild sheep. A change from this nomadic to the
sedentary life occurred in the Neolithic period; men began to
till the soil, they raised oxen, cows and sheep and they dwelt in
circular or rectangular houses built of raw brick and occasionally
of stone.

The copper objects brought to light in the settlements of
Shengavit, Kültepe and Garni are markedly similar to those
found in the Royal Cemetery at Ur of the Chaldees. The

13

chalcolithic culture which embraced the entire extent of the Armenian highlands is closely related to the contemporary culture of the neighbouring lands in Western Asia, in the Caucasus, Iran and Mesopotamia. The pottery has the characteristic black burnish and its ornamentation consists of geometric designs.

The Bronze Age in Armenia extended from the middle of the second millennium to the tenth century BC. Among the objects belonging to this period one should mention a gold bowl from a tomb, decorated with three pairs of confronted lions. To this period also belong the numerous dolmens, menhirs and cromlechs that are a feature of the country. The fishshaped stones known as *vishaps* (the Armenian word for dragon) are a special type of megalith of which specimens also exist in Georgia. On some are carved the head and forelegs of an ox, on others birds and even a human figure. These megaliths are usually found on hills, close to the sources of lakes or streams, and they were probably associated with some form of water cult. This is also suggested by the sinuous lines simulating water carved on some of the *vishaps*. Fragments of other *vishaps* were hollowed out to form water conduits, and they probably formed part of a highly developed irrigation system.

The earliest written records concerning the inhabitants of the territories which were to form part of Armenia are found on the Hittite tablets from Boghazköy. The annals of Suppiluliumas (*c.* 1388–1347 BC) and those of his son Marsilis I (*c.* 1347–1320) recount the wars waged against the dynasts of the neighbouring small kingdoms of HayasaAzzi and further south against the people of Suhma, Ishuwa and Alshi.

With the fall of the Hittite empire the sources of information about these tribal groups disappear. The Assyrian annals refer to the people of Nairi, a coalition of minor kings in the region south of Lake Van, who were defeated by the Assyrian ruler Tukultininurta I (*c.* 1255–1218 BC). Tiglathpileser also led

Plate 4

Fig. 2

Fig. 3

expeditions against them (1115 BC and 1114 BC). In the inscription discovered at Yončalu, about 30 km. distant from Manazkert (Mantzikert), Tiglath-pileser calls himself the conqueror of the lands of Nairi. This is the oldest inscription found on the soil of Armenia.

There is no further mention of Nairi, until the resurgence of the Assyrian kingdom in the ninth century BC. Ashur-nazir-pal asserts with pride that he destroyed two hundred and fifty towns of Nairi which covered an area that extended as far as the land of Urartu. We have here the first mention under this name of what was to become one of the powerful realms of the Near East. The earlier Assyrian inscriptions of the thirteenth century used the form Uruatri; the Biblical form of the name is Ararat, while the people themselves called their land Biani(li).

The Urartians appear to have been one of the tribal groups of Nairi, of Hurrian extraction, who gained ascendancy over the others and organized a strong central state. Shalmaneser III (860–823 BC) waged war against them intermittently throughout his reign. The reliefs on the famous bronze gates from Balawat, now in the British Museum, show episodes of his victorious campaigns, the destruction of the town of Sagunia of 'Aramu the Urartian' and the capture of the fortress of Arzashku. In 834 BC, Shalmaneser led an expedition against the Urartian king Sarduri whose capital was at Tushpa, that is the actual city of Van.

During the reign of Sarduri's son, Ishpuini, and those of his successors Menua, Argishti and Sarduri II, the Urartians consolidated their power. In the eighth century Urartian rule extended over the region between Lake Van and Lake Urmia, as far north as Transcaucasia, and to the west as far as North Syria. Urartu then became the largest state in Western Asia, and its control of the trade-routes to the Mediterranean was a serious threat to the Assyrian economy. Urartian wares were exported to Phrygia, to the mainland of Greece and some have

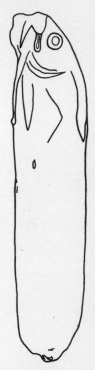

Figs 2, 3   Vishaps *nos 2 and 5 found at Imirzek (after Marr and Smirnov)*

even been found in Italy. Argishti built the fortress palace of Erebuni, on the plain of Ararat, the name of which is still preserved in Erevan, the capital of Armenia, and he founded the important administrative centre of Argishtihinili, also in the plain of Ararat.

The situation changed in the late eighth century, when Tiglath-pileser III and especially Sargon II invaded Urartu, sacked several towns and inflicted heavy losses on the army. There was a short period of recovery under Argishti II and Rusa II, evidenced by the foundation of new towns, in particular Teishe-baini, near Erevan, now known as Karmir-blur.

But the central power gradually weakened, through inner struggles, the dissatisfaction of the allied groups, the mass flight of slaves, as well as through the inroads made by the Cimmerians and the Scythians. Urartu survived but a few years after the downfall of Assyria, in 610/609 BC. The Medes destroyed the capital of Tushpa, while some years later they entered the plain of Ararat, seized Teishebaini and took over the entire region.

By the end of the seventh century Urartu, incorporated in the empire of the Medes, had disappeared from the historical scene, but during the centuries of its existence it had been a great nation, the centre of a culture whose importance and significance is being increasingly recognized as scientific explorations bring to light its monuments and artistic products. The Urartians excelled in large public works. The inscriptions record the numerous fortresses, towns, temples and palaces built by Menua in the late ninth and early eighth centuries BC; of these there only remains to this day a canal 70 km. long, which brought water from the mountain to Tushpa-Van, but the constructions of his successors have fortunately been revealed in different parts of ancient Urartu. At Erebuni (Arin-berd) the central, peristyle hall was surrounded by rooms and other halls; in the south-west of the peristyle hall lay the palatine temple. The fragments of the

Figs. 4, 5 Figures on a bronze helmet of Sarduri II. Erevan, Armenian Historical Museum (after Piotrovskii)

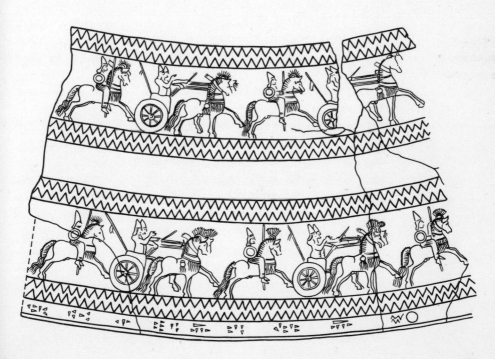

wall paintings in red and dark blue on a white ground reveal an art close to Assyrian in style. Erebuni appears to have been abandoned and some of its treasures carried to Teishebaini (Karmir-blur) which after its foundation by Rusa II became the administrative and economic centre of Transcaucasia. The citadel with the palace of the governor covered an area of about 1600 sq. m.; the walls built of mud brick on a substructure of heavy masonry rose to a height of 7 m. and the general aspect of the projecting towers and walls with their crenellated parapets can be surmized from the bronze model of a building found at Toprak-kale. There were about 150 rooms on the ground floor; some of these still had giant storage-jars for wine or grain. In a room decorated with wall paintings, one of the jars contained ninety-six bronze cups. The objects found in various parts of the buildings comprised bronze shields, helmets, belts, quivers and other objects of military equipment, many of them decorated *Figs. 4, 5* with reliefs of animals, representations of gods, warriors, sacred trees and so forth. These and the bronzes found at Toprak-kale such as the ornamental figures of winged lions which probably formed part of a decorated throne, as well as the ivories from Plate 3 Altintepe, and the statuettes and gold jewellery found on different sites, show the high quality of an art allied to that of Assyria, but having its distinctive features, for the Urartians display a more marked tendency to schematize the human, animal and plant forms. The large bronze cauldrons with four bull's heads around the rim are a characteristic Urartian type, and they were exported to other countries, probably as far west as Italy.

The excavations in the western and southern areas of Urartu, in particular those at Altintepe, near Erzinjan, at Kayalidere, in the Mush area, and at Patmos, north of Lake Van, have supplemented the knowledge derived from the results obtained at Arin-berd and Karmir-blur. Foremost among these discoveries come the remains of temples, the general aspect of which was hitherto known primarily through the picture of the

Musasir temple on the reliefs from Khorsabad. These temples were square structures with buttresses at the four corners surrounded by a paved court with a line of columns. The ceremonial hall (the *apadana*) with three rows of columns found at Altintepe was decorated with paintings on each of its four walls, and three other painted rooms formed the north side of an entrance court. The stone-built tombs found on this same site consist for the most part of a vestibule and a room of offerings which preceded the tomb chamber; the bodies were either laid directly on the floor or buried in stone sarcophagi.

All these discoveries are important for the later artistic history of Armenia, but so far the connecting links are not apparent, for no thorough investigations have yet been made in areas where the successive layers of the soil can show a continuous occupation of the site from the Urartian to the Armenian period.

CHAPTER II

The History of Armenia

THERE ARE NO historical records concerning the original home of the Armenians, an Indo-European people. The initial stages of their settlement in the Kingdom of Urartu and of their amalgamation with the local population remain equally obscure. The earliest mention of the Armenian people, as Armenoi, occurs in the writings of the Greek historian Hecataeus of Miletus (*c.* 550 BC); some thirty years later their country is designated as Armina in the inscription of Darius I at Behistun (Bisitun). In a part of the Book of Jeremiah, which modern scholarship dates *c.* 594 BC, the prophet calls together, against Babylon, 'the kingdoms of Ararat, Minni and Aschchenaz' (LI. 27). At that time Urartu (= Ararat), incorporated into the Median empire, was no longer a separate kingdom, but its name persisted, for the Babylonian version of the Behistun inscription has Urartu in the place of Armina.

According to Herodotus the Armenians had migrated from Phrygia into Armenia, and their armour was the same as that of the Phrygians (VII. 73). In the fourth century Eudoxus, as quoted by Stephanus Byzantinus in his *Ethnica*, also refers to their common origin with the Phrygians; he adds that the languages spoken by these two groups of peoples were similar. Modern Armenian historians tend to underrate the testimony of Herodotus and to give greater importance, where the formation of the Armenian nation is concerned, to the Hayasa-Azzi group on the upper course of the Euphrates, and to the Armeni-Shubria who inhabited the region lying to the west of Lake Van.

The migration of the Armenians towards the Euphrates must have taken place in several stages and it seems probable that coming from Phrygia they mingled with the people of Hayasa-

Azzi; then, taking advantage of the weakening and final destruction of Urartian power, they gradually settled in Urartu and imposed their language, an Indo-European tongue, on the local population.

Armenian tradition has preserved several legends concerning the origin of the Armenian nation. The most important of these tells of Bel and Hayk—the eponymous hero of the Armenians who call themselves Hayk', and not Armenians. The historian Moses of Khoren relates that Hayk, a descendant of Japheth, Noah's son, revolted against the titan Bel after the destruction of the Tower of Babel; taking with him his entire family numbering some three hundred persons, and also other men, he went to the land of Ararat, situated to the north. On his way he stopped by a mountain, subjected its inhabitants, and founded an establishment which he gave to his grandson Armenak, the son of Cadmus. Pursuing his route to the north-west, he reached a high plain called Hark' where he built a village which he named Haykashen (built by Hayk). Upon hearing of Hayk's disobedience Bel sent his son with a message summoning him to obey his orders. Hayk refused, whereupon Bel, gathering his forces, marched against him. The encounter took place close to a salt water lake (Lake of Van); an epic battle was fought between the two armies of titans, but Hayk, who was a consummate archer, shot an arrow which pierced Bel right through his chest. At the death of their leader, Bel's army took to flight. In memory of his victory Hayk built a village which he called Hayk', the region was called Hayots' dzor (valley of the Armenians) and the nation was named Hayk' after its ancestor Hayk. Moses of Khoren then goes on to speak of Hayk's descendants whose names were given to the different provinces and cantons of Armenia; he relates at some length the valiant deeds of Aram whose fame extended far beyond the limits of his country. Consequently the neighbouring nations called the people Armens or Armenians.

According to Strabo, the Armenians first settled in the district of Acilisene (present Erzinjan) and in the area around the source of the Ziban-Tigris; from there they proceeded eastward as far as the Calachene and Adiabene. At a fairly early date they must have penetrated the interior and occupied the Armenian plateau. After the collapse of the Urartian Kingdom the country fell under the rule of the Medes and later under that of the Achaemenids. Some Urartians probably still formed a distinct group, for Herodotus includes the Armenians in the 13th satrapy of the Achaemenian empire, while the Urartians and other Hurrian remnants formed the 18th satrapy. By 401–400 BC, when Xenophon and the Ten Thousand passed through these lands, the entire basin of the western Tigris and that of the Euphrates/Arsenias probably lay within the boundaries of Armenia. In what Xenophon calls Armenia, namely the region west of the Centrites, Orontes was ruler; but Tiribazus ruled in the district north of the Taurus (western Armenia).

In the *Anabasis* Xenophon also gives some information about the social order of the country. The clans constituted the basic institution, while their chiefs ruled over the fortified rural settlements which were surrounded by walls and ditches. These tribal elders or *comarchs* had charge of the local administration, the satrap being responsible for the entire country. Part of the tribute paid to the Persians took the form of horses which, according to Xenophon, were smaller but more fiery than those of the Persians. Agriculture was considerably developed, for in all the villages the Ten Thousand found abundant supplies of wheat, barley, green vegetables, various oils and wines. They were feasted with lamb, goat-flesh, pork, veal and fowl, different kinds of bread and a special beverage, made with barley, which they drank through a straw. The people lived, together with the cattle, in underground dwellings with a narrow opening at the top, through which they entered by means of a ladder; there were separate entrances for the cattle. In one of the villages

Xenophon saw the house of the satrap surrounded by many others with towers.

Despite its romantic character, specific information can also be gleaned from Xenophon's *Cyropaedia*. His long account of Cyrus's relations with the king of Armenia, of the judgement scene at which the king's eldest son, Tigranes, a close friend of Cyrus's, intervened on his father's behalf, are no doubt, by and large, figments of Xenophon's imagination. There is nevertheless an historical core in these stories, for Tigranes is also known to Moses of Khoren, and he can be identified with the son of the Armenian ruler Orontes.

The pioneer work of the late Professor Manandian, followed by the studies of S. Eremian, G. Tirats'ian and C. Toumanoff have thrown light on one of the most obscure periods of Armenian history, namely the centuries immediately preceding the rule of the Artaxiad dynasty in 189 BC. It has now been established that the Orontids, a family of Achaemenian descent, ruled in Armenia as satraps from *c.* 401 BC on, and after 331 BC as kings, at times under Seleucid suzerainty. The names of most of these dynasts have been preserved in the inscriptions of the commemorative monument of Nimrud Dagh, erected by Antiochus I of Commagene, himself a scion of the same Achaemenian family.

Hellenistic influence penetrated Armenia during the Orontid period, and the Greek language was used by the upper classes of Armenian society. Greek inscriptions have been found at Armavir, the first Orontid capital, founded in the Ararat valley on the site of the ancient Urartian town of Argishtihinili. These indicate the existence of a Greek temple of Apollo and Artemis, served by a predominantly Greek priesthood. One inscription, found in 1927, has been interpreted as bearing an address from Mithras, high priest of the Temple of the Sun and the Moon, to his brother, King Orontes IV, while another alludes to the king's tragic death.

During the reign of Orontes IV the royal residence was transferred from Armavir to a rocky promontory close to the confluence of the Akhurian and Arax rivers. The new capital was called Ervandashat after the name of its founder Ervand, the Armenian form of the name Orontes. This city was fortified with high walls, and within these walls the rock was hewn out in many places to the level of the river in order to allow water to flow into these cavities for the use of the inhabitants. Iron staircases led to the bronze gates of the citadel, and into these staircases walls and traps were built as a safeguard against any attempt against the king's life. All the treasures of Armavir were brought to Ervandashat, but the idols were lodged in a small town built further north on the left bank of the Akhurian river. This town was named Bagaran, meaning the city of the gods or idols; Eruaz, the king's brother being appointed high priest. Orontes-Ervand also planted a large forest to the north of the river, stocking it with numerous animals for the chase.

The foundation of several other towns by the Orontids is to a large extent connected with the development of commerce and the changes introduced into the economy of a country which hitherto had been primarily, or one might say exclusively, agricultural. One branch of the important trade route which connected Central Asia with the Black Sea and the Mediterranean passed through the plain of Ararat, and such cities as Armavir and Ervandashat probably served as focal points for the commerical relations. No coins minted by the Orontids of Armenia have come to light, but the considerable number of drachmas and tetradrachms of Alexander, the gold staters and the Seleucid coinage found on Armenian soil, are indicative of a developing economy and of increasing trade with neighbouring countries.

Orontid rule came to an end at the close of the third century BC. A local dynast, Artashes (Artaxias), who in the Aramaic inscription found at Zangezur, in the province of Siunik', also claims to be of Orontid descent, revolted against Orontes, defeated him, seized the capital Ervandashat, and became master of the greater part of the Orontid realm. Following the defeat of Antiochus III at the hands of the Romans in the Battle of Magnesia (190 BC) Artashes proclaimed himself an independent king. Although his attempt to seize the neighbouring kingdom of Sophene, after the death of its ruler Zariadris, proved unsuccessful, the kingdom of Artashes covered almost the entire Armenian highlands, extending from the Euphrates on the west, almost to the Caspian Sea, and from the Caucasus in the north to the Taurus mountains.

The new capital Artashat (Artaxata) 'the joy of Artashes', was situated on the Arax river at its confluence with the river Metsamor. Strabo speaks of the beauty of the site on a peninsular-like elbow of land. The river surrounding the walls of the city added to its protection except at the isthmus, which was enclosed by a trench and a palisade. Plutarch has maintained a tradition, also known to Strabo, according to which Hannibal the Carthaginian had gone to the court of Artaxias after the battle of Magnesia. Having found in the country a pleasant, but neglected and unoccupied site, he drew up plans for a city, which he encouraged the king to build. The king, greatly pleased, asked Hannibal to oversee the work and thus a large and stately city was erected. Many modern historians have accepted Plutarch's story, although there is no other record concerning Hannibal's sojourn in Armenia. The statues of Artemis and of all the other pagan divinities were transferred to Artashat from Bagaran, save that of Apollo which was erected on a road outside the city.

The Armenian monarchy reached its apogee under the reign of Tigran the Great. Held as a hostage at the court of the Parthian kings, Tigran was released in return for the cession of seventy valleys in the neighbourhood of Atropatene. His first act, after his ascension to the throne in 95 BC, was to seize the small kingdom of Sophene. Two of the separate kingdoms of the Armenian territory were thus reunited; as for the third, that of Lesser Armenia beyond the Euphrates, it had been annexed by Mithridates Eupator of Pontus. The treaty of alliance and friendship signed by the two rulers was sealed by the marriage of Tigran with Cleopatra, the daughter of Mithridates. The internal troubles in Persia, following the death of Mithridates the Great, provided Tigran with the opportunity to recover the valleys he had been obliged to cede; in victorious campaigns undertaken between 88 and 85 BC he further extended his conquests, occupying northern Mesopotamia and imposing his suzerainty on the minor rulers who had been under Parthian overlordship. After the peace treaty with the Parthians, Tigran assumed the title of 'King of kings' hitherto held by the Parthian rulers. Next, turning his arms against the western countries, he occupied Northern Syria, advanced into Phoenicia and Cilicia, and also seized several Cappadocian cities. By the year 70 BC, Tigran had become one of the most powerful rulers of the Near East, and his vast empire extended from the Caspian to the Mediterranean and from the Caucasus to Palestine and to Cilicia.

The older Armenian royal residences being too far removed from the newly acquired possessions, it was necessary to found a more central capital. This was Tigranocerta, and its site has been identified by some scholars as that of the medieval town of Martyropolis (modern Farkin or Mayafarkin), at the foot of the Taurus mountains, on the north bank of the Tigris. It was thus situated at a midway point of Tigran's empire, in close proximity to the Achaemenian royal road, and connected, in various directions, with the important commercial centres.

Tigran did not spare any effort in fortifying and adorning his capital. According to Appian the city walls, which rose to a height of 50 cubits, were so wide that storehouses and stables had been built in them; strong walls also protected the citadel.

Like all Hellenistic cities, Tigranocerta had a theatre in which Greek plays were performed. A magnificent palace was built outside the ramparts, surrounded by gardens, hunting grounds and other places for enjoyment. In order to people his new capital, Tigran made the inhabitants of twelve Greek cities that he had destroyed move into it; several Greek scholars came of their own accord and Tigranocerta became the principal centre from which Hellenistic culture spread into Armenia. The population also included many members of the Armenian nobility, and Plutarch reports that every common man and every man of rank sought to adorn the city in imitation of the king.

Rome had maintained a neutral position during Tigran's victorious campaigns, but it did not long remain aloof, for the establishment of a powerful foreign empire ran contrary to Roman ambitions and, moreover, threatened its own recently acquired possessions in Asia Minor. Having first defeated Mithridates Eupator of Pontus, Rome turned its arms against Tigran. The excuse seized upon was Tigran's refusal to deliver Mithridates, who had sought refuge at his court. In a rapid, secret march the Roman armies invaded the Armenian territories and Lucullus laid siege to Tigranocerta. The forces hastily assembled by Tigran were defeated, the Greek mercenaries opened the gates of Tigranocerta to the Romans and the city was mercilessly plundered by the soldiers. For the celebration of the triumphal games Lucullus made use of the players whom Tigran had invited for the opening of his theatre.

The fall of Tigranocerta dealt Tigran's empire a mortal blow, for all the western lands that he had conquered now accepted Roman suzerainty. On their own native ground, in the Armenian highlands, Tigran's forces were able to hold in check the armies of Lucullus and inflict some losses on them, but when a fresh expedition was sent under Pompey, Tigran, after a desperate resistance, finally had to sue for peace (66 BC).

27

What had been a vast empire was now reduced to the purely Armenian territories placed under the hegemony of Rome.

The establishment of Roman power in Asia Minor created a political situation which was to affect the future history of Armenia. The country now became a buffer state between two mighty and rival empires, the Roman and the Iranian. This still applied when Byzantium succeeded Rome and when the Arabs conquered Persia. Each one of these empires sought possession of the natural bastion formed by the Armenian highlands. By dominating the valley of the Euphrates the eastern powers had easy access into Asia Minor, while the valleys of the Euphrates and of the tributaries of the Tigris provided a convenient route for the western powers into Iran and Meso/potamia. In addition to these strategic advantages, control of the Armenian forces, especially of a cavalry renowned for its valour, brought a noteworthy addition to the military potential of each of the opposing armies. Finally, by supporting in turn the different political parties within Armenia, her neighbours encouraged the latent rivalries of the feudal lords, rivalries which by weakening the central power of the king were one of the factors contributing to the loss of national independence.

After the dethronement of the last of the Artaxiad rulers at the close of the first century BC, foreign kings were appointed sometimes by Rome, at other times by the Parthians, as the fortunes of war favoured now one, now the other country. The Peace of Rhandeia (AD 63) created for a time a *modus vivendi*. Trdat, the brother of the Parthian king Vologases, whom the latter had appointed as king of Armenia, was recognized by Rome and became the founder of the Arsacid dynasty. Accom/panied by an escort of 3000 cavalrymen, he journeyed to Rome where he was crowned by Nero in the course of a great ceremony held in the Forum (AD 66). Trdat was allowed to rebuild the ancient capital of Artaxata; Roman architects, sent by Nero, took part in this reconstruction.

The war which flared up anew between Rome and Iran had its usual repercussions on the fate of Armenia. The situation became much more critical when the Sasanians overthrew the Parthian kingdom (AD 226) and invaded Armenia. The destruction of their Parthian kin and the murder of their own king brought a rapprochement between Armenia and Rome. Trdat III, who had taken refuge in Rome, was appointed king of Armenia (*c.* AD 287). The forty years' truce signed at Nisibis (AD 298) between Rome and Iran, brought a much needed respite during which the country tried to heal the wounds caused by the invasions and the wars fought on her soil. A new capital was built at Dvin, near the river Azat, a tributary of the Arax, and the greater part of the population of Artashat was transferred there. King Khosrov also planted a large forest, on either side of the river Azat, which he stocked with numerous animals.

Hardly had the period of truce ended, when the Iranian king Shapur II invaded Mesopotamia and entered Armenia. With only brief interruptions the war continued for fifty years. Throughout these centuries of perpetual warfare, in which the Armenian armed forces had played a major role, the constant aim had been to maintain the integrity of the territory as well as some degree of national independence. The descendants of the Arsacid family had occupied the royal throne almost continuously; they had directed the internal affairs of the realm and the social feudal order had remained unchanged. The power of the Church had grown after Christianity had been established as the state religion in the early fourth century, and its leaders had played an important role in the affairs of the realm. The situation was to change after the peace signed between Byzantium and Iran in AD 387.

By virtue of this treaty Armenia was divided into two vassal states subject to the Byzantine and Sasanian empires respectively. Persia was in the ascendancy at the time and acquired the greater part of the country, that is all the provinces which lay east of a line which passed from Theodosiopolis (Erzerum) in the north, to Martyropolis (Mayafarkin) in the south. In Byzantine Armenia, King Arsaces III retained nominal power; no successor was named after his death and the country came under the supervision of the *Comes Armeniæ* and later under that of the *Magister militum per Armeniam*. In Persian Armenia an Armenian king retained nominal power until 428, but after the death of the last member of the royal house the country was administered by the *marzpan* or margrave appointed by the Persian king. A second partition of Armenia occurred in 591 following a new war between Persia and Byzantium at which time the latter, being more powerful, received the larger share; the line of demarcation between the two parts now extended roughly from Tiflis in the north to Dara in the south, passing by Dvin, Maku and the Lake of Urmia.

Conditions in general differed considerably as between the two sections. Byzantine policy was directed toward the destruction of the feudal system of the Armenians and the centres of national resistance constituted by the *nakharars*, that is, feudal lords; it aimed to extend the Byzantine system of administration to these lands which now formed part of the empire. The emperor Zeno abolished the hereditary transmission of power of the *nakharars* to the eldest son; he ordained that they should henceforth pass to men of the emperor's choosing, just as was the rule for the other offices of the empire. Justinian introduced further changes. Byzantine Armenia, known as Armenia IV, was placed under the authority of a governor of consular rank. Two edicts, promulgated in 535 and 536, granted to the daughters equal rights with the sons; moreover, they entitled the daughters to a dowry. Consequently the feudal domain was dismembered and the power of the head of the house greatly diminished.

In Persian Armenia the rulers respected the existing social and political organization. Even after the replacement of the king by a *marzpan* they did not attempt to modify the feudal system which was akin to the one prevailing in their own country. No changes were introduced into the hereditary laws, the *nakharars* retained many of their old privileges and prerogatives, they continued to raise their own cavalry, but as vassals of the Persian king they were under obligation to place their troops at his service in time of war. Several of the *marzpans* were chosen from among the members of the Armenian nobility. These favourable conditions were due to the relative weakness of the Persians, but gradually their rule became more oppressive, and a process of 'Iranization' of the country was attempted mainly through the channel of religion. The growing dissatisfaction of the Armenians culminated in open revolt when Yazdgard III demanded that they renounce the Christian faith and accept Mazdaism; the Church, the nobility and the people rallied around the commander-in-chief, Vardan Mamikonian. They determined to put up armed resistance, despite unfavourable circumstances—part of the cavalry being with the Persian army engaged in fighting against the Huns, and the request to send armed assistance having been refused by Byzantium. After minor engagements in which the Armenians, assisted by Georgian and Albanian contingents, were successful, the decisive battle was fought in the plain of Avarayr, on May 26, AD 451. The historian Eghishe has described in moving terms the epic encounter between the overwhelming forces of the Persians, including the select troop of the 'Immortals' mounted on their elephants, and a small army of determined men fighting for their faith and for their independence. The night before, which was the Eve of the Pentecost, had been spent in vigil, the catechumens in the army had been baptized and had received Holy Communion. Despite their valour and their determination, the small Armenian forces, further depleted by the defection of the Iranophile *nakharars*, were defeated. Vardan Mamikonian, the flower of the Armenian nobility and very many valiant men fell fighting. The names of all the leaders have been recorded by the historians and they are commemorated, as martyrs of their faith, at the annual service performed in Armenian churches.

Though defeated on the battlefield the Armenian revolt had not fully subsided and guerilla warfare continued in the mountainous regions.

The revolt of the Georgian king Vakhtang Gorgaslan, who called upon the Armenians to assist him, was the spark which kindled a fresh uprising in Armenia. In a secret gathering Vahan Mamikonian, a nephew of Vardan, and all the feudal lords took a solemn oath to join forces against the common enemy. The war which started in AD 481 continued with varying fortunes until 484. The Persians, who had suffered a crushing defeat in their war against the Huns, were obliged to come to terms with the Armenians. Freedom of religious worship was restored, the rights and privileges of the feudal lords were recognized, and Vahan Mamikonian was named *marzpan*. During the years of his office and those of his immediate successors Armenia was virtually a vassal state. However, after 555, Persians were again appointed as *marzpans*. The peace of 591 signed between Byzantium and Persia resulted in the second partition of Armenia referred to above.

The chapters devoted to Religion, to Literature and Learning and to the Arts will show that these troubled years and the first half of the seventh century, were nevertheless a productive and creative era. The advent of the Arabs on the political scene seriously altered the general situation. Their incursions began in 640 and in 652 the Armenian general Theodore Rshtuni was forced to recognize Arab suzerainty.

With the resumption of the war between Byzantium and the Arabs, towns and provinces passed, time and again, into the hands of the rival empires; the situation was further complicated by the dissensions among the *nakharars,* some of whom favoured the Byzantines, while others sided with the Arabs, who at first had seemed more liberal masters than the Greeks. The Syrian historian Dionysius of Tell Mah're, who passed through Armenia in 716/17, states that the country, once remarkable for the number of its inhabitants, the abundance of vineyards, cereals and magnificent trees, was now devastated and deserted. Arab rule became more oppressive when the Abbasids overthrew the Umayyad dynasty and the revolts were ruthlessly repressed. Many *nakharars,* taking with them their families and followers, sought refuge in the Byzantine territories. This mass exodus had the most serious consequences. Not only were the people deprived of some of their natural leaders and protectors, but the abandoned lands were seized and populated by Muslim immigrants. Thus a number of Arab emirates came into existence; these constituted barriers to the unification of the country, once it had been liberated from the foreign yoke.

War between the Arabs and Byzantium had been resumed in the middle of the ninth century and the successes of the Byzantine armies favoured those who, like the Armenians and the Georgians, chafed under Arab oppression. The Armenian revolt of 851 had been put down after a long and desperate struggle, and all the *nakharars* had been carried as captives to Samarra. But with the victorious advances of the Byzantine armies, fear of new uprisings compelled the Arabs to adopt a more conciliatory policy towards the Armenians. In 861 the caliph liberated the *nakharars* and he appointed Ashot Bagratuni as 'Prince of princes of Armenia, Georgia and the lands of the Caucasus', a title which carried with it the right to levy taxes.

The Bagratunis were the leading feudal family at the time. Having not taken part in the Armenian revolt of 774–5, they had retained their lands and their position. The caliphate needed the help of the Bagratunis against the Arab emirs of Armenia who were striving to become independent. Harun ar Rashid had therefore granted the title of Prince of Armenia to the head of the house, and he had appointed the younger brother general of the Armenian forces. From then on the Bagratunis gradually enlarged their possessions, and their domain extended from Taron in the south-west of Armenia to the provinces of Shirak and Arsharunik' in the north. After his appointment as Prince of princes, Ashot further strengthened his position. At the death of the head of the Mamikonian family he took possession of the province of Bagrevand. Through alliances with the Artsrunis of Vaspurakan and the lords of the eastern province of Siunik' he established friendly relations with them. Moreover he had the moral support of the head of the Church, the Catholicos, whose residence was on his domains. In 885/6 the assembly of the *nakharars* and of the Catholicos elected him king of Armenia. The caliph confirmed this election by sending a crown, although he still considered the Armenians as his vassals and continued to exact a tribute. Ashot had been cautious enough to keep aloof of the war between Byzantium and the Arabs, and shortly after his election he received a crown also from the emperor Basil I, himself an Armenian.

The monarchy, thus restored after a lapse of more than three centuries, was nevertheless faced with serious difficulties. These came to a head when Smbat (890–914), who lacked the wisdom and ability of his father Ashot, ascended the throne. The Artsrunis of Vaspurakan, rivals of the Bagratunis, held vast domains which extended from the province of Ayrarat in the north, to the Lake of Urmia in the south-east. Ashot had gained their support, but an unpolitical act of Smbat destroyed the alliance: he ceded to the prince of Siunik' the city of Nakhitchevan which was within the province of Vaspurakan. Incensed by this, Gagik Artsruni sought the assistance of Yusuf, the emir of Azerbeijan and the avowed enemy of King Smbat. Nothing could have been more welcome to the Arabs than this demand for help, since one of the constant aims of their policy had been to encourage the enmities between the feudal families in order to weaken the authority of the central power.

Upon the recommendation of Yusuf, the caliph conferred a crown on Gagik in 908, and the region of Vaspurakan thus became a separate kingdom, the first of several which were to be created in the course of the century. Yusuf and Gagik joined forces and defeated the royal armies (914). Yusuf killed Smbat after subjecting him to cruel tortures, and he sent the body to Dvin to be nailed on a cross. Not content with this victory, Yusuf's armies continued to fight, in order to destroy the Bagratid kingdom, and they might have succeeded had it not been for the courage and energy of Smbat's son Ashot II who succeeded him. Many of the *nakharars* rallied around their king, and Gagik himself, repentant of his rash deed, withdrew from his alliance with Yusuf. In the guerilla warfare which lasted for several years the Armenians were assisted by their Iberian and Albanian allies. The Iberian king Adarnase placed the crown on the head of Ashot, just as he himself had received it earlier from the hand of Ashot's father. A rapprochement with Byzantium was brought about principally through the inter-mediary of the Catholicos John, the historian, who was in correspondence with the patriarch Atticus and the emperor Constantine Porphyrogenitus. Upon the emperor's invitation Ashot went to Constantinople and was received with great honours, returning laden with presents, and what was more im-portant, accompanied by a Byzantine contingent. Ashot and his allies were successful in their fight against the enemy forces as well as against the unruly *nakharars,* and the Arabs were forced to give in. Ashot received a crown and the title of King of kings. This made him in theory the suzerain of all the other rulers in Armenia, and after their reconciliation Gagik agreed to be known only as king of Vaspurakan.

In effect, however, the Bagratid king was little more than a *primus inter pares* and his authority rarely extended beyond the limits of the royal domains. The feudal organization of Armenia was at the same time its strength and its weakness. Renowned for their courage, jealous of their independence, the *nakharars* defended their possessions with the utmost energy. These centres of resistance prevented the occupying forces from having complete control of the country. Had the *nakharars* been able to unite and subordinate their private ambitions to the common interest they would have saved their country from many disasters, even if ultimately they could not have opposed the overwhelming forces of their powerful neighbours.

The custom of creating apanages for younger sons was a second cause of weakness. Partly through these provisions, partly through the acts of the princes who raised their principalities to the rank of kingdoms, the country was fragmented into a number of separate states. In 961 Ashot III allowed his brother to become king of Kars, ceding to him the province of Vanand. He gave to his third son the district of Tashir and surrounding regions. In 982 these constituted a separate kingdom with the town of Lori as its capital. Towards the end of Bagratid rule, what remained of the royal domain was divided between the two brothers Ashot IV and John-Smbat III. In 968 the kingdom of Vaspurakan was divided between three brothers. To this list of separate states should be added the principality of Taron, and that of Siunik' which had been raised to the rank of a kingdom.

Despite these divisions, the tenth and early eleventh centuries were, by and large, a peaceful and prosperous era. The Abbasid rulers, hard pressed by the Byzantine armies, were not in a position to seriously interfere in Armenia; the local Muslim emirs had accepted the Bagratid suzerainty, and the invasions by the neighbouring Muslim dynasties, in particular the Hamdanids, had no lasting effects. The internal situation gave reason for greater concern. The nobility, the merchant class and the artisans had benefited from the revival of commerce, but in the country the free peasantry had greatly diminished. The large landowners, including the important monasteries, tended to absorb the holdings of the small proprietors, thus reducing the peasants to serfdom. There were a number of popular uprisings, in particular in the province of Siunik', where the wealthy monastery of Tat'ev had acquired, through purchase or by donation, a number of villages. The peasants refused to give up their land; they attacked the monastery, and could only be subdued after the repeated intervention of the armed forces of the prince of Siunik'. Serious disturbances were also occasioned by the heretical sect of the T'ondrakets'i, whose doctrine had much in common with that of the earlier sect of the Paulicians. The T'ondrakets'i spread to several provinces of Armenia in the course of the tenth and eleventh centuries, and they found many adherents among the common people. These, no doubt, saw in some of the tenets of the doctrine, such as the rejection of the regular practices and sacraments of the Church and, especially, in the rejection of the authority of the clergy, an expression similar to their own opposition against the wealthy hierarchy. Secular authorities joined with the Church in persecuting them, but remnants of this sect long survived.

The long reign of Gagik I (989–1020) marked the apogee of Bagratid rule; Armenia was at peace and prosperous, and the king embellished Ani with new buildings. The capital had been transferred in 961 to this city, situated on a high plateau, *Fig. 6* protected on the east and south-east by the deep ravine of the Arpa Tchai (Akhuryan), a tributary of the Arax, and on the west by the valley of the Aladja-Tchai, the 'valley of the flower-gardens', which joined the Arpa Tchai. The growth of the city had been so rapid that less than forty years after the construction of the boundary walls a second line of fortifications was built, Plate 2 almost trebling the area of the capital. Palaces and numerous churches were erected, so that Ani came to be known as the city of a thousand and one churches.

Gagik's death was followed by a rapid decline. The rivalry between his two sons ended in a partition which further reduced

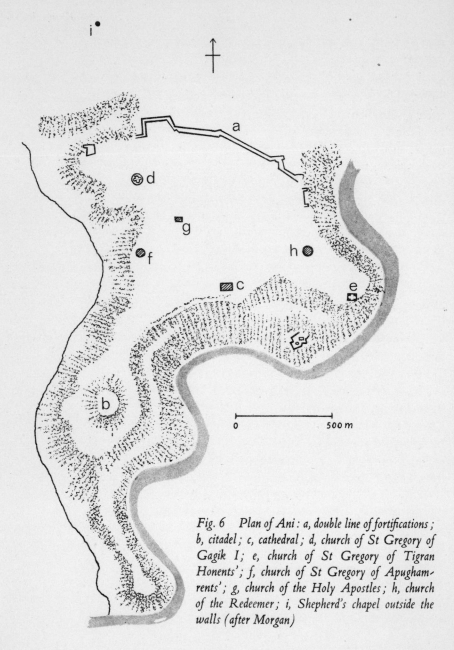

Fig. 6 Plan of Ani: a, double line of fortifications; b, citadel; c, cathedral; d, church of St Gregory of Gagik I; e, church of St Gregory of Tigran Honents'; f, church of St Gregory of Apugham-rents'; g, church of the Holy Apostles; h, church of the Redeemer; i, Shepherd's chapel outside the walls (after Morgan)

the royal domain. The absence of a strong hand at the helm, the lack of unity among the different kingdoms and principa, lities, proved fatal at a time when the Byzantine policy of annexations was making rapid progress, and when a powerful enemy, the Seljuk Turks, had risen in the east. In 966/67 Byzantium had annexed the principality of Taron; Byzantine forces, under the authority of an imperial military commander were thus installed in a strong position in the south, west of Armenia. With the acquisition of the domains of David II, this Iberian Bagratid's Armenian possessions also passed into Byzantine hands; they comprised the province of Apahunik', north of Lake Van, with the city of Mantzikert as its capital. In 1021/22 the king of Vaspurakan, hard pressed by the Seljuks, ceded his kingdom to Basil II. This cession was followed by a mass exodus of the king's vassals and retainers and large sections of the population. Thus all the eastern and southern provinces of Armenia formed part of the Byzantine empire. The other kingdoms were now in a dangerous situation and could not hope to hold out for long against Byzantine pressure, either direct or indirect.

The Bagratid king, John Smbat III, fearful of reprisals for his assistance to the Georgian ruler, designated Basil II as his heir. After his death the claims of the Emperor were supported by pro, Byzantine elements in Ani, acting primarily through personal ambition. In the struggle which lasted for two years the national party finally triumphed. The Byzantine armies were repulsed, and the young prince Gagik was crowned king (1042). During three years he fought valiantly against the Byzantine forces and those of the emir of Dvin, whom Byzantium had incited against him, and he repulsed the incursion of the king of Lori. Deceived by enemies both at home and abroad, he was lured to Constantinople and forced to abdicate. The resistance of the population of Ani and its leaders was of no avail; Byzantine forces soon took possession of the city and of the entire kingdom. Soon after, Gregory Magistros ceded his principality to Byzantium and in 1064 King Gagik of Kars was forced to do likewise. Only the small kingdoms of Lori and Siunik' retained a semblance of independence. The imperial policy of annexations, fateful for Armenia, also spelled disaster for Byzantium. The Empire was not in a position to replace by sufficient armed forces the Armenian armies that had been disbanded, and the way now lay open for the march of the Seljuks into the vital provinces of Asia Minor. Seljuk invasions of Armenia, begun in 1048, continued with increasing force. Ani fell in 1064, so did Kars, which had not remained long in Byzantine hands. After the Byzantine disaster of Mantzikert in 1071 all Armenia was under Seljuk rule.

The rise of Georgian power, begun under King David IV (1089–1125), known as 'The Builder', culminated during the reign of his great-grand-daughter, Queen Tamara (1184–1213). After freeing their own land from the Seljuks, the Georgian rulers advanced into Armenia. The liberated areas included the territories of the kingdoms of Ani, Kars, Lori, the principalities of Bjni and Siunik', and also the important city of Dvin. In short, the entire northern, central and eastern provinces of Armenia were now under Georgian suzerainty and the direct control of Armenian or Armenized feudal lords. The Zak'arians, the commanders-in-chief of the Georgian and Armenian armies, were the most powerful among this new nobility, their fiefs included the Ararat plain with Ani as their seat, and the region of Lake Sevan. The Orbelians, who had held a similar position, were the masters of the province of Siunik'. A number of other feudal lords were the vassals of these two main ruling families. During the latter part of the twelfth century and the first quarter of the thirteenth, until the arrival of the Mongols, Armenia was virtually independent, and flourishing. Following the example of the earlier *nakharars,* the new nobility, as well as rich merchants like Tigran Honents' of Ani, endowed the monasteries, and erected religious and secular buildings. Literary activities, which had been somewhat in abeyance during the Seljuk occupation, were revived and continued even during the Mongol period.

Destructive as were the Mongol invasions, which began in 1220 and ended by the occupation of Armenia in 1236, the internal situation was not seriously affected at first. Armenia, like Georgia, was now a vassal of the Great Khan, and owed him tribute and armed service. The princes who had gone to the Mongol court were reinstated in their feudal right, but they were obliged to go to the court whenever summoned. Having become part of the vast Mongol empire, Armenia benefited from the current active international trade, and economic conditions gradually improved. But the northern cities of Dvin, Ani and Kars no longer held the foremost position, for the southern route along the north shore of Lake Van appears to have been used more often. The lands under Mongol domination enjoyed religious freedom, and persecutions started only when the Mongols were converted to Islam.

Thus, by and large, Armenia was to some degree independent during the thirteenth and part of the fourteenth century. There were cordial relations between the Mongols and the Armenian nobility. Several Armenian princes were present at the election of Güyük as Grand Khan in 1246. The historian Vardan visited the Mongol court several times and he was specially invited by Hulagu to the great assembly of July 1264. Another historian Stephen Orbelian, archbishop of Siunik', witnessed the christening of Khan Arghun's son, and he was asked to bless the chapel sent by the Pope. Armenians, familiar with the eastern languages, often acted as interpreters. Prince Smbat of Siunik' spoke Georgian, Uigur, Persian and Mongol. At the Mongol camp, the Franciscan missionary William of Rubruck found 'Hermenian priests who knew Turkish and Arabic', and at the court of Mangu he met an Armenian monk by the name of Sargis who helped him 'with the language'. The alliance between the Mongols and the Armenian kings of Cilicia also favoured these friendly relations.

Despite these contacts, the Armenian princes were not in a position to prevent many of the lawless acts and the exactions of the Mongol chieftains, who interfered increasingly in local affairs. A special tax was imposed after the census taken in 1254 and the Mongol hand lay heavy on the population. The wars waged by the Mongols, in which the Armenians had to take part, deprived the country of all its able-bodied men. Conditions deteriorated even more when, with the weakening of Mongol power, the different nomad tribes, in particular the Turkomans, penetrated in larger numbers into the country, dispossessing the Armenian peasants. The final blow came with the devastating invasion of Timurlane at the close of the fourteenth century. All vestiges of national independence henceforth disappeared.

In the preceding pages frequent references were made to the Byzantine conquests and annexations of Armenian lands, and to the large numbers of inhabitants who settled in the Byzantine territories either through emigration or through deportations. The role they played in the affairs of the empire is essentially part of Byzantine history and it has been studied in a number of important articles and books. But it also constitutes one of the significant chapters in the history of the Armenian people and should be considered here, at least briefly.

The Armenians were one of the most important and influential ethnic groups in the heterogeneous population of the Byzantine empire. They were a dominant element in the army both numerically and by virtue of the valour of their contingents and leaders alike. Procopius mentions sixteen Armenian generals in the armies of Justinian, in addition to the famous general Narses. An even larger number held prominent positions in the armed forces during the eighth–eleventh centuries, and Byzantium owed its victorious campaigns against the Arabs primarily to the great skill of such Armenian generals as Petronas, the brother of the empress Theodora, and especially John Curcuas (Gurgen). The chief naval commander during the reign of Romanus Lecapenus, Alexius Musele, was also an Armenian.

Armenians held important positions in the administration. Several were appointed governors of provinces, and more than one ascended the imperial throne. Beginning with Heraclius, and for several centuries thereafter, most of the great emperors were Armenians. The so-called Macedonian dynasty was an Armenian dynasty, for Basil I, although born in Macedonia, was an Armenian. During the tenth century even the usurpers— Romanus Lecapenus, Nicephorus Phocas, John Tzimisces— were wholly or partly Armenians. In fact almost every major figure in the administration was of Armenian descent, so much so that some modern historians refer to the ninth and tenth centuries as the Graeco-Armenian period. During the eleventh century members of several Armenian families continued to hold prominent positions in the Byzantine administration.

Armenians also played a role in the intellectual life of the Empire. The Caesar Bardas, brother of the empress Theodora, whose decade of administration (856–866) has been considered as one of the most brilliant in Byzantine history, re-established the University of Constantinople, housed in the palace of the Magnaura, thus laying the foundations for the splendid revival that took place in the ninth–tenth centuries. He entrusted the direction of the University to another Armenian, Leo the Philosopher or the Mathematician, a man of encyclopaedic knowledge. Leo's uncle, John the Grammarian, the iconoclast patriarch from 837 to 843, was another Armenian reputed for his erudition.

Thus Armenians contributed to the greatness of Byzantium in diverse fields. The greater opportunities offered by the vast and powerful Empire enabled them to play a much more important role than had been given to any Armenian in his own country.

CHAPTER III

The Kingdom of Cilicia

IN THE SECOND HALF of the tenth century, after the re-conquest of Cilicia and of Northern Syria by the Byzantine emperor Nicephorus Phocas, Christian immigrants—of whom the Armenians formed the largest contingent—were settled in the towns and fortresses from which the Muslim population had been expelled. By the end of the century, the Armenians were sufficiently numerous in these parts to warrant the appointment of a bishop at Tarsus and of another at Antioch. Fresh Armenian immigrants arrived in the course of the eleventh century, some from Cappadocia, where they had accompanied the kings and minor rulers who had been granted domains within the terri-tories of the empire in return for their kingdoms that had been seized; others directly from Armenia, after the Seljuk conquest.

Fig. 7
The establishment of the Armenians in Cilicia opened a new chapter in their history. For the first time they were in a country with a direct outlet to the sea, and they came into contact with new nations. For their settlement in Cilicia coincided with the Crusades and the creation of the Latin kingdoms and principa-lities of the Levant. Because of this new situation, and these new contacts, the civilization which developed in Cilicia differed in several respects from that of the mother country.

Two Armenian families held key positions in Cilicia. The Het'umids, the masters of the forts of Baberon and Lambron in western Cilicia, commanded the southern egress of the Cilician Gates and the route which led from the Anatolian plateau directly to Tarsus in the Cilician plain. Vassals of Byzantium, to whom they remained faithful, they came repeatedly into conflict with the other feudal family, that of the Rubenids. The latter, who were established in the mountainous region east of the Cilician Gates, with their principal seat at Vahka, were

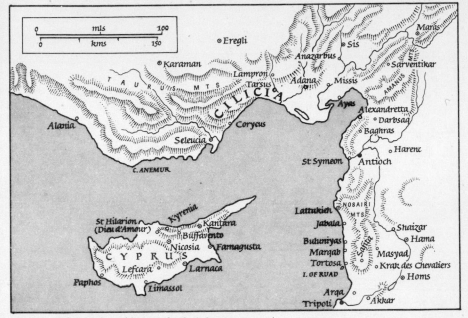

Fig. 7 Cilicia and neighbouring lands (after Runciman)

far more ambitious politically and aimed to gain control of the land. The history of the first hundred years is dominated by the attempts of the Rubenids to descend from their mountain strongholds to the arable lands of the Cilician plain, to seize the cities on the trade routes, and to reach the coast. In order to protect themselves from the attacks of their north-western neighbours, the Seljuks of Iconium, the Rubenids tried to have complete control of the Cilician Gates and this became a source of conflict with the Het'umids. The attempts of the Rubenids to safeguard their eastern borders by controlling the passes of the Amanus mountains engendered warfare with the princes of Antioch. They had, moreover, to guard against the encroach-ments of other Latin rulers who sought to enlarge their possessions at the expense of the Armenian chieftains. But throughout this period Byzantium, to whom Cilicia still belonged, was the principal adversary.

The inroads made by the successors of the first Rubenids, T'oros I (1100–29) and his brother Leo I (1129–37), who had seized several cities in the plain, alarmed the Byzantine court. An expedition led by John Comnenus recovered these cities, and on its way to Syria completed the reconquest of Cilicia in the winter of 1137–38. Leo, his wife and their two sons were carried as captives to Constantinople and Armenian rule in Cilicia seemed for ever lost. A second chapter of the struggle opened a few years later when T'oros, the younger son of Leo I, escaped from Byzantium. T'oros rallied around him the Armenians of the eastern section of Cilicia and, assisted by his brother Stephen and his cousin Joscelin, count of Edessa, succeeded in regaining part of his lost possessions. Armenian control extended once again into the Cilician plain, and once again Byzantium reacted. When indirect measures had failed, Byzantium sent a strong expeditionary force, prepared with the utmost secrecy in 1158; it took T'oros by surprise and triumphantly marched through the Cilician plain. The consequences of the Armenian defeat were, however, less serious this time. T'oros, having submitted, was allowed to retain his mountain strongholds, and the Armenian barony of Cilicia was re-established under Byzantine suzerainty. Despite his reverses T'oros had laid the foundations on which his successors were to build. Ruben III (1175–87) progressively seized the cities of the plain which the depleted Byzantine forces of Cilicia were no longer in a position to defend. The occupation of the entire territory, extending from Isauria on the west to the Amanus range in the east was completed by Ruben's brother Leo II, during whose reign the barony was raised to the rank of a kingdom. In 1198, Leo was crowned in great solemnity in the cathedral church of Tarsus. He was anointed by the Armenian catholicos and he received from the hands of the papal and imperial legate, Conrad, archbishop of Mainz, the royal insignia sent by the Roman emperor, Henry VI. The Syrian Jacobite patriarch, the Greek metropolitan of Tarsus, other ecclesiastical dignitaries and numerous feudal lords, among them several Greeks and Franks who held possessions under Armenian suzerainty, were present at the ceremonies. The Byzantine emperor also recognized the elevation of Leo I by sending him a crown.

The change of status from a barony to a kingdom and the organization of a strong Christian realm, hailed by the Armenian writers as the restoration of their ancient kingdom, was also important from the European point of view. For the position of the Latins of the Levant had been seriously weakened by the Muslim conquests. Edessa having been captured in 1144, the county was destroyed shortly after. Jerusalem had fallen in 1187 and the three large cities of Antioch, Tyre and Tripoli were hard pressed by Saladin. Leo ensured unity within his realm by destroying the power of the Het'umid lords of Lambron. Through his second marriage, and those of his daughter and his niece, he established useful alliances with the kings of Cyprus and of Jerusalem and with the Byzantine emperor of Nicaea. By granting territories to the military orders of the Hospitallers and of the Teutonic Knights, he gained their assistance in the defence of his frontiers. In order to stimulate commerce he opened the ports of Cilicia to the merchants of the Italian republics, granting special privileges to the Genoese, to the Venetians and to the Pisans. He was less successful in his wars against the Seljuks of Iconium, but he succeeded nevertheless in maintaining the integrity of his territories.

Leo had the ambition to found a Franco-Armenian state by gaining control of Antioch. With this end in view he had contracted a marriage between his niece and heiress presumptive, Alice, and Raymond, the eldest son of Bohemond of Antioch. Raymond having died before his father, his son Raymond-Rupen became Bohemond's heir and was crowned prince of Antioch in 1216 at the death of his grandfather. The rights of

Raymond-Rupen were however contested by Bohemond of Tripoli, a younger son of Bohemond of Antioch, and after a war which lasted for three years Raymond-Rupen was ousted. Too many difficulties lay in the way of the realization of Leo's ambitious project. Had his plans succeeded, the establishment of a Christian state, more powerful than any of those existing in the Levant, might have been instrumental in turning the tide of history.

Leo's reign and the greater part of the joint rule of Leo's daughter Zabel (Isabel) and Het'um I (1226-69) were periods of prosperity and of power. The marriage of Zabel and Het'um, the son of Constantine of Lambron, sealed the alliance between the two rival families, the Rubenids and the Het'umids. It also brought to the throne a scion of a cultured family, the Het'umids, more interested than the Rubenids had been in intellectual and artistic pursuits.

The Mongols, whose hordes had·swept through Armenia and Georgia far into Anatolia, constituted the most serious threat at the time. Realizing that only an alliance with them could save his kingdom, Het'um sent his brother, the Constable Smbat, on a special mission to Karakorum in 1247. The brief account of this journey is known through the letter written by Smbat to his brother-in-law, Henry I of Cyprus, a letter trans-mitted by William of Nangis in his *Vie de saint Louis*. Het'um himself visited the Great Khan Mongka in 1253; he was the first Christian ruler to come to the Mongol court of his own accord, and he repeated his visits to the court of the Ilkhans after the capture of Baghdad by the Mongols. The Armenians, having recognized Mongol suzerainty, were obligated to give them military assistance and to pay a tribute, but they were entirely free in all their internal affairs; moreover, they had the promise of Mongol assistance in the protection of their own kingdom. In seeking Mongol friendship Het'um also had larger aims in mind. He believed that only with their help could the Christian states of the Levant offer adequate resistance to the Muslims and ultimately defeat them. He therefore tried to win the Latin princes to the idea of a collaboration with the Mongols. But he could only convince his son-in-law, Bohemond VI of Antioch, who together with the Armenians, participated in the war against the Ayubid sultans, and entered Aleppo and Damascus with the Mongol armies.

The Mongol alliance proved beneficial so long as their armies were victorious, but the Armenians experienced its counter-effects when Mongol power weakened in Syria, and when Cilicia became one of the principal targets of the Sultans of Egypt. With but short periods of respite, Mameluk attacks gained in intensity during the latter half of the thirteenth century. The armed forces that the Armenians could muster were greatly inferior to the powerful Egyptian armies. Time and again Cilicia was invaded, the cities of the plain were pillaged, and only in mountainous regions were the Armenians able to offer effective resistance, though even these strongholds could not always be adequately protected. In 1292 the citadel of Hromkla, the see of the catholicos, fell after a siege of thirty-three days; the catholicos was made a prisoner, the precious relics and treasures assembled in the church and the patriarchal residence were looted or destroyed. Whilst the Mongol alliance, revived by Het'um II, and the friendly disposition of Ghazan towards the Christians although he had adopted Islam, awakened fresh hopes for a while, the successors of Ghazan were more fanatical, religious persecutions began, and the Armenians could no longer rely on Mongol help. With the collapse of Outremer, Cilicia was now in the front line and the way lay open to the Mameluk armies. The port of Ayas (Lajazzo) which by the importance of its trading activity rivalled the ports of Syria and of Egypt, was partly destroyed in 1322. Renewing their attacks in 1337, the Mameluks demanded that the fortifications of the port be razed, and Ayas lay henceforth at their mercy.

Internal strife further weakened the Armenian realm. Fratri-
cidal wars between the brothers of Het'um II, rivalries among
the barons, and antagonism between the pro-Latin and anti-Latin
parties created a situation which could only profit the enemy.
The religious controversies were at the root of this antagonism.
Just as the Byzantine rulers had tried to enforce Orthodoxy on
the Armenians, so also the Papacy wished to bring about their
submission to the Roman Catholic Church. The Franciscan
missions were active in Cilicia and made many converts,
principally among the members of the nobility and even some
of the royal family. Het'um II himself had donned the Franciscan habit. Some of the leading ecclesiastics also favoured
closer connections with the Roman Catholic Church. These
conversions and submissions to the demands of the Papacy
caused a rift between the Cilician kingdom and the mother
country where the episcopacy and the monks of the leading
monasteries were the staunch defenders of the national traditions.
They also led to conflict in Cilicia itself, for the majority of the
population and many of the leaders remained faithful to the
national Church.

The frictions between the pro-Latin and anti-Latin parties,
so detrimental to the welfare of the state, increased in 1342 when
in the absence of a male heir the throne passed to Guy de Lusignan, the son of the Armenian princess Zabel and Amalric of
Lusignan, king of Cyprus. Several rulers followed one another
in quick succession, brought to the throne by the rival parties.
In the meantime enemy armies continued their raids, capturing
the cities of the Cilician plain. As in the early period of their
settlement, the Armenians were driven back to their mountain
strongholds. Finally in 1375 the capital, Sis, fell to the Egyptians
and the last king, Leo V (VI), was taken as a captive to Egypt.
He was released after seven years through the intervention of
John of Castile and Peter of Aragon. He died in Paris in 1393
having sought in vain to interest the Western rulers in the

recovery of his throne. His tomb is now in the abbey church of Saint Denis, next to those of the French kings.

These are the main outlines of the turbulent history of a kingdom established with high hopes in a new land and which finally succumbed under the impact of overwhelming forces. During the course of the relatively brief existence of this kingdom, its history had become a part of European history. The Armenian rulers had participated in the common cause of Christendom and together with the kings of Cyprus they had continued to fight after the disappearance of the Latin kingdoms of the Levant. Het'um I had dreamt of an alliance of all the Christians with the Mongols, in order to recover the Holy Land, and in the early fourteenth century his namesake and relative, Het'um or Hayton, prince of Corycus, advocated the same cause. In 1307, while Hayton was at a Praemonstratensian abbey near Poitiers, he composed upon the request of Pope Clement V his book entitled *La Flor des Estoires de la Terre d'Orient*, a book which he dictated in French to Nicolas Falcon and which the latter translated into Latin. In the fourth chapter of his work Hayton outlined a plan for a new crusade. He recommended that a double expedition, sent by sea, be based in Armenia and Cyprus, and establish an alliance with the Mongols. The Crusader and Mongol armies were, however, to fight separately in order to avoid possible conflicts between them. The time had long passed when such a project could have been put into execution, but it expresses the hopes that the Armenians continued to cherish.

This work composed in French, the letter of the Constable Smbat and his translation of the Assizes of Antioch testify to the spread of the French language, and with it of Frankish customs among the Armenian nobility. This was to a large extent a result of the family alliances established from the early twelfth century on. These alliances had begun with Armenian princesses marrying Baldwin I of Boulogne and Baldwin II of

Rethal, the first kings of Jerusalem, and they continued in the following centuries. There is, in fact, hardly an important Crusader family that did not intermarry with the Armenians. Several of the Rubenid barons, and later the kings of Armenia wedded Frankish ladies of high birth.

The cosmopolitan character of Cilician society was further strengthened when Frankish barons, the members of the Military orders, the Franciscan missionaries and merchants of different nations all took their place in it. Definite information is lacking concerning the number of Greeks who continued to reside in Cilicia after it had ceased to be part of the Byzantine empire, but they must have been fairly numerous, for they had their own churches and their own clergy, presided over by the Greek patriarch. Finally, there were the Syrian Jacobites who owned their own monasteries and with whom the Armenian clergy maintained very friendly relations. The presence of all these foreign elements and the continued contacts with the Latin principalities awakened an interest in the past history of these nations. In 1210 Het'um, prince of Lambron, translated from the Latin two brief works; one, entitled the Series of the Roman emperors, lists the Western rulers from the Emperor Augustus to Philippe Auguste, King of France, the other gives the succession of the pontiffs of Rome from Saint Peter to Innocent III. An important section of the Chronicle composed in the late thirteenth century by the historian Het'um (Hayton) contains a list, together with brief information, of the Roman emperors, the popes, the Merovingian and Capetian kings, the Ottonian emperors, the kings of Sicily, Germany and England. His principal source for this work appears to have been the Chronicle of the Dominican writer Martin the Pole, also known as Martin of Bohemia. Nerses, archbishop of Lambron, translated the rules of St Benedict and the Latin Ritual which had been brought by the Armenian bishop sent as a legate to Pope Lucius. Nerses also translated the Ritual of the Anointment of the Kings which the Archbishop of Munster had brought with him when he accompanied Frederick Barbarossa. These works are of an entirely different order from those which in the past had been translated from Greek or Syrian. The latter included philosophical treatises, the writings of the Church Fathers, works of real significance. The translations from Latin do not include any important book, they are works of limited scope, which served to acquaint the Armenians of Cilicia with the bare outlines of the history of the people who now formed part of the Cilician community.

CHAPTER IV

Society and Economics

INFORMATION concerning the social and political organization of Armenia in the Achaemenian period is scanty and the gradual process which culminated in the fully developed feudal system at the time of the Arsacid rulers is difficult to reconstruct. Various elements of this system are already apparent during the rule of the Artaxiad dynasty, and it outlived the destruction of the Armenian monarchy, especially in the sections of the country occupied by the Persians and later by the Arabs.

Foremost in the hierarchic order were the four *bdeashkh (vitaxae)*, the hereditary viceregal lords and defenders of the frontier regions in which they held vast domains. They are no doubt to be identified with the four kings, who, according to Plutarch, were in constant attendance on Tigran the Great, and who published his decrees to the people. The *bdeashkh* are no longer mentioned after the fall of the Arsacid dynasty, and their role must have lapsed with the abolition of the monarchy.

Next in rank came the *nakharars*, the hereditary heads of the princely houses. They constituted the most important group in the social system, and they played a decisive role in the political history of the country. Their patrimonial domains were autonomous states which under the laws of primogeniture passed to the eldest son, or to the younger brother should the older one die before his father, or be incapacitated. The rights of the women were recognized in the rare instances in which there were no direct male descendants, or no males in the senior line. The kings recognized the inalienable rights of the *nakharars*, for even when they seized the lands of the latter, for some reason, they did not appropriate them but they returned them to the heirs of these *nakharars*. Within their domains the *nakharars* enjoyed fiscal, judiciary and administrative powers, they raised and controlled their armed forces. They took an oath of fealty to the king, an oath taken over salt, and the king promised them protection in return for their services. There was also a ceremony of investiture, when the insignia consisting of a diadem, a signet ring and perhaps a banner as well, were presented to the *nakharar*. The services which the *nakharars* owed to the king consisted primarily in furnishing cavalry troops in time of war. They were bound to guard some of the king's castles and if necessary to allow the king to garrison his troops in their own castles. The king could also demand monetary aid in addition to the military assistance given by the *nakharars*. On special occasions the king called the *nakharars* in assembly to seek their advice.

The *nakharars* participated in the court life and ceremonies and held important offices some of which were hereditary. The office of coronant, already mentioned in the Aramaic inscription of Artashes found at Zangezur, became the apanage of the Bagratuni family. The Mamikonians were the commanders in chief *(sparapet)* of all the armed forces of the realm. The Gnunis were in charge of the finances and of the rural economy; their title was that of *hazarapet* but their functions were less important than those of the Sasanian *hazarbadh* who was the prime minister of the kingdom. The Grand Chamberlain *(mardpet)*, also called the King's Father, was in charge of the king's estate, of his fortresses, his treasures and the administration of the court. This office was always held by a eunuch.

In theory all the *nakharars* were equal but in practice there were differences between them; the terms senior or junior *nakharars* used by the historians are usually connected with the importance of their domains and the size of the army they could muster. Their order of precedence at court was established according to a system. The Throne-List *(Gahnamak)* which purports to give this order, is unfortunately a compilation of late date, and there are divergencies in the lists transmitted by the historians whenever they name the *nakharars* called in council by the king or assembled in a church council. The order of precedence must have varied from time to time, according to the fortunes of the specific houses, the only stable element being the relative importance among the different groups, which agrees with the designations of senior or junior *nakharars*. The Military Register *(Zoranamak)*, a list of the military potential of the different principalities, is also a relatively late compilation. However, comparisons with information provided on various occasions by the contemporary historians have shown it to be fairly accurate. On the basis of these different sources, modern historians have calculated that the most powerful *nakharars* could muster up to 10,000 horse and that the smallest contingent consisted of 100 horse. During the Arsacid monarchy the size of the cavalry varied from 70,000 to 120,000 men, a far from negligible army; in the Arab period these forces dwindled considerably.

The *sepuhs* came after the *nakharars* in the social order. They were the princely cadets, originally co-possessors of the dynastic *allodia*. After the fall of the Arsacid monarchy they were allotted apanages out of the communal patrimonies.

The freemen *(azats)* constituted the minor nobility. Holders of small fiefs, they were the vassals of the king or of the *nakharars*, and they formed their cavalry troops. Many of the court officials were selected from among them. They participated in the administration of the princely domains and, on occasion, they were called for consultation by the *nakharars*, just as the latter were invited by the king. They were subject to taxation but were exempt from corporal punishment.

The *ramiks* were the lowest order in the feudal system. This general term includes both the poor class of city dwellers and the peasants *(shinakans)*. The shinakans were attached to the soil as serfs although they were personally free. They could own a few animals, and their agricultural implements. Their material conditions varied greatly; while many lived in great poverty, others had acquired some wealth for there are references to property that they had bought. They formed the basic taxable population, paying also the ecclesiastical tythe. They owed the corvée to their masters, in exchange for the land they tenanted; they took part in all public works such as the construction of roads, bridges, fortresses and so forth. In time of war the *ramiks* formed the infantry; they were enrolled without pay and they had no share in the spoils. Some of them were horsemen, but their companies were distinct from the cavalry of the nobles.

The urban population, especially the artisans and traders, many of whom were foreigners, enjoyed greater freedom. The large cities had special rules of government and raised their own militia. Very little is known about the slaves except that their number was comparatively small; they were for the most part war prisoners and to a lesser degree persons sold in settlement of debts.

The organization of the Church had marked affinities with the feudal system. The clergy was included in the class of freemen *(azats)*, the priests received fiefs *(k'ostaks)* from the bishop or from the abbots of large monasteries in return for the church services. These fiefs were hereditary, like those of the nobles, but should the holder commit some grave fault, the fief returned to the Church. Initially the dignity of the Catholicos, or supreme head of the Church, had become the apanage of the family of Gregory the Illuminator, and the members of the episcopate were chosen from among the nobility. The see of the Catholicos was in the royal domain. The episcopal sees corresponded to the important princely states and they bore the same territorial title.

The Catholicos was the supreme judge of the realm; bishops and priests performed the duties of judges in minor cases. During the greater part of the Middle Ages the only written codes were the rules and regulations established in various Church councils, and the collection of canons made in the eighth century by the Catholicos John of Odzun, and incorporated in the Corpus of Canon Law *(Kanonagirk')*. The canons of the Church councils, in particular of the one held at Shahapivan in the fifth century, included several clauses pertaining to laymen, but there must have been, in addition, an oral tradition relating to cases which were not covered by these canons. The Book of Laws or Book of the Tribunals *(Datastanagirk')* composed in the late thirteenth century by Mkhit'ar Gosh is, to a large extent, a compilation of these written and unwritten laws. This work, the first and only complete Armenian code, was also used outside Armenia. It was adopted and translated into the vernacular of Cilicia by the Constable Smbat, the brother of King Het'um I. The Armenians who had migrated and settled in Poland in the fourteenth century obtained by royal decrees permission to be judged according to their national laws, as codified by Mkhit'ar Gosh, and his Book of Laws was later translated into Latin (1518) by order of King Sigismund. It was translated into Mongolian for the Armenians of the Crimea and in the eighteenth century, King Vakhtang VI of Georgia incorporated sections from it into his Code.

The feudal system of Great Armenia was modified in the kingdom of Cilicia under the impact of contacts with the Franks. The feudal lords, now called barons (a word which has passed into modern Armenian to denote Mister) were no longer the hereditary heads of their autonomous state. As liegemen they owed homage to the king and the tenure of their fiefs was regulated by the same laws as those of Western Europe. The authority of the Cilician king over his barons was thus greater than had been the case in Great Armenia. There the king was the *primus inter pares*; the title of 'King by the grace of God' which the Cilician kings bear on their coins and in their charters, a title never used in Armenia, is in itself indicative of the difference.

European nomenclature was adopted in Cilicia for several high officers of the realm and the offices themselves were sometimes new creations or modifications of the former ones. The chief magistrate was the Chancellor, called *chantsler* (transcribed in accordance with the pronunciation of the Armenians of Cilicia); under his authority were grouped the special chancellors, the interpreters and translators, for French and Latin were often used by the chancellory, especially in the charters granted to the commercial companies. The bailiff *(bayl)* was the lieutenant or regent of the kingdom and he ruled the country during the king's minority. The officer in charge of the management of the royal palace and estates was now called the seneschal *(sinichal)*, and the generalinchief of the Armies was designated as the Constable *(kuntsdabl)* instead of *sbarapet*. The marshall *(marachakhd)* was under his immediate orders. The chief baron *(avak baron)*, who presided over the royal council, enjoyed great authority. Some of the Byzantine titles, such as *sebastos, pansebastos,* which had been conferred at the time of Byzantine suzerainty were maintained, as was the designation of *proximos* for the minister of finances. The kings of Cilicia also revived the office of coronant *(t'akatir)* which appears to have lapsed during the Bagratid rule.

As mentioned above, the Constable Smbat had adapted the Law Book of Mkhit'ar Gosh, but in matters pertaining to the feudal class the Armenians appear to have followed Western usages, as may be seen from a passage in the Assizes of Jerusalem. The bailiff Constantine wished to give to his younger son, Oshin, the castle of Corycus which he had received from the king. His eldest son, the Constable Smbat, contested his right to thus dispose of the castle, whereupon Constantine sought the advice of John of Ibelin. The latter answered that the donation to Oshin was valid, for Constantine was free to dispose of a castle received as a gift, and Smbat had to abide by this decision. The same Constable Smbat reports that, as Frankish customs had penetrated into Cilicia, it had become necessary to have an Armenian version of these laws, and he therefore translated the Assizes of Antioch, used in Cilicia in preference to the other codes. This Armenian translation is a most precious document, since the original text of the Assizes is lost.

The order of knights was introduced at a fairly early date in imitation of the Frankish customs. While he was still a baron, Leo had been knighted by Bohemond III, prince of Antioch. When the barony was raised to the rank of kingdom, the Armenian rulers themselves conferred this honour on their own subjects and even, on occasions, on other princes. Thus in 1274, Bohemond VII, the last prince of Antioch, was knighted by King Leo II (III). Great festivities accompanied these ceremonies. In 1256 Het'um, wishing to knight his eldest son Leo, invited for this occasion his sister, the Countess of Jaffa, his sons-in-law Bohemond VI, prince of Antioch and count of Tripoli, and Julian, lord of Sidon, together with their wives, as well as many dignitaries of his realm, and members of the clergy.

Historical writings and the discourses of religious authors shed some light on the daily life of the Armenian nobility. Hunting was their favourite pastime. In the vicinity of the towns they had built, the Artaxiad and Arsacid rulers had planted large forests where they kept wild animals. Falcons were used in the sport of hawking, and the Armenian falcons were much sought after. The theatre was another pastime. Pantomimes, comedies, various songs and dances were performed, attracting large crowds who went to the theatre, say the ecclesiastical writers, in preference to going to church. Mimes, musicians, and dancers were always present at the banquets of the nobles, and the bards most probably sang some of the pagan and epic poems of which fragments have been preserved. At one of these festive occasions at the Artsruni court, the prince himself, wishing to entertain his guests, took the lyre from the hands of one of the musicians. So great was the nobles' love of entertainment, that at times they even went to the monasteries accompanied by their singers and dancers. Many are the criti-cisms addressed to the nobles for their intemperance and their excesses of all kinds. In Cilicia, tournaments became the fashion, in imitation of the Franks. Willebrand of Oldenbourg, who visited Cilicia in 1211, describes the ceremonies of the blessing of the waters at the feast of Epiphany. The king rode on a high horse between the Master of the Teutonic Knights and the Master of the Hospitallers' castle of Seleucia, accompanied by the men of their orders. Next came Prince Ruben surrounded by the nobles and soldiers carrying banners, and followed by the Armenian clergy and the Greek patriarch bearing sacred vessels. The entire company came to the shore of the river, where the cross was dipped into the waters. After this ceremony there were great festivities, when jousts, tilts and other acts of prowess were performed by the nobles.

In their palaces, kings and nobles tried to compete with the sumptuousness of the courts of their suzerains, and they adopted the costumes of the latter. Procopius describes the costume of the hereditary satraps. Their cloak, made of the wool of the Pinnos, a bivalve which grows a silky beard, was fastened with a golden brooch from which hung three saphires held by loose golden chains. Gold overlaid the part of the cloak in which the purple cloth is usually inserted and gold decorations also adorned the silk tunic. The satraps wore red boots reaching to the knees 'of a sort which only the Roman Emperor and the Persian King were permitted to wear'. These various items of ceremonial attire often took the form of gifts made by the suzerains. When Vasak, prince of Siunik', went to the Persian court he donned the robe of honour which he had received from the king, he tied the diadem and put on the golden crown, he girded a massive gold belt studded with pearls and other precious stones, he put on his ear-pendants and collar and threw his sable cloak around

his shoulders. The portraits of kings and princes, executed in
sculpture and painting, give us some idea of the rich garments
they wore.

Plates 36, 55

In Cilicia the kings and nobles abandoned the Persian and
Arab fashions and adopted the costumes of the Franks. This
change had taken place as early as the late twelfth century, as
can be seen from a letter addressed by Archbishop Nerses of
Lambron to Leo I (II). Nerses, who had been criticized for
introducing Latin customs into church ceremonies, wrote:
'Just as you have ordered us to conform to the traditions of our
fathers, follow likewise those of our ancestors. Do not go bare-
headed like the Latin princes and kings, who, say the Armenians,
have the appearance of epileptics, but wear the *sharpash* like your
forefathers; let your hair and beard grow like them. Don the
wide and woolly *tura*, instead of the mantle and close-fitting
tunic.' These statements are corroborated by the portraits of
Cilician rulers on their coins and in manuscripts. Like many
other medieval rulers, the Cilician kings also followed Byzantine
models for their ceremonial vestments and they are represented

Plate 74

wearing the typical Byzantine chlamys.

The secular buildings of Armenia have all been destroyed,
but the description of the palace King Gagik Artsruni had
erected on the island of Aght'amar gives us some idea of how
sumptuous were its appointments. The main hall was surrounded by numerous vaulted exedrae and square rooms, all
of them richly decorated; it was crowned with a high dome, of
which the gold shone with brilliant light. In this palace the
artists had represented 'gilt thrones on which the King is seated
in elegant majesty, surrounded by brilliant-faced young men,
attendants of his rejoicings, also by groups of musicians and
young girls dancing in an admirable manner. There are represented also companies of men with bared swords and combats of
wrestlers; groups of lions and also wild beasts; flocks of birds of
rich and varied plumage.' These scenes depicted in fact the

favourite pastimes of the rulers and of the nobility. Other chronicles mention, in passing, the rich hangings on the walls and the doors of the palaces and the costly vessels used by some of the nobles.

Women had their own quarters in the palaces and the dwellings of the wealthy, but they were not shut away and they participated in the social life. They attended the theatre, and were often present at the banquets given by their husbands, especially during the early centuries. No woman ever reigned alone in Armenia or in Cilicia, but in a few instances the queen governed the realm for a short period in the absence of the king or during the minority of their son after the king's death. At times they acted as ambassadors or intercessors. Thus in 851 when Yusuf invaded Armenia and marched against Ashot, prince of Vaspurakan, the latter asked his mother Hrip'simē to carry his letter to Yusuf. Hrip'simē was successful in her mission and peace was temporarily established. Women controlled a certain amount of wealth and owned property. Numerous inscriptions mention their donations of farms and villages to monasteries. Several churches were entirely erected with the funds provided by women; they also offered precious vessels and hangings, some of which they themselves had embroidered. In 1191 the wife and daughters of one of the feudal lords presented to the monastery of Getik an altar veil embroidered in many colours with scenes of the life of Christ and portraits of saints.

The churches, monasteries and palaces built by the kings and feudal lords, and the costly vestments worn, are the outward signs of the prosperity enjoyed by the upper classes when the country was not ravaged by wars and invasions. But we should not be giving an accurate picture of life as a whole if we omitted to record the condition of the lower classes. The chronicles give only scant attention to this aspect, but scattered references show the great poverty of the masses even in periods of prosperity. More information can be gleaned from the collections of proverbs of the thirteenth century in which the life of the rich and poor are contrasted. At all times, and not only during foreign occupation, the latter were overburdened with taxes. The peasant revolts which broke out time and again were the direct result of the impoverishment of the peasantry. Those who fled to the cities did not fare any better. The excavations of Ani have shown the inadequacy of the houses in which they lived and many persons, we are told, sought shelter in caverns. As trade developed, various forms of usury came to be practised and men and children were sold into slavery.

Trade formed the principal basis of Armenian economy. The reign of Tigran the Great, before the Roman victories, was a most prosperous period, as can be seen from the accounts of Plutarch. He relates that when Lucullus seized Tigranocerta he found eight thousand talents of coined money in the treasury and he distributed eight hundred drachmas to each soldier out of the spoils of the city. When peace was concluded with Pompey, Tigran paid a contribution of six thousand talents.

At no time in the following centuries was Armenia so well placed either politically or economically, but the geographic position of the country favoured the development of a transit trade. During the Parthian period the main route to the Mediterranean passed south of the Caspian Sea and entered Syria by way of Ecbatana, Ctesiphon, and Seleucia. But there was an overland route to the Black Sea through northern Mesopotamia and Armenia along which many merchants travelled. The foundation of new cities in Arsacid Armenia coincides with the development of world trade in the Roman and Byzantine periods, and Armenians took part in these exchanges as middle-men. Artaxata is one of the three cities mentioned in the imperial edict of 408–409 at which, by agreement between Byzantium and Sasanian Persia, international trade could be carried on. Theodosiopolis and Dvin in the north, and Nakhitchevan in the south, on the road from Ecbatana to Artaxata, were other important trade centres. Procopius speaks of the numerous merchants who conducted their business at Dvin and in the surrounding villages. 'For from India and the neighbouring regions of Iberia and from practically all the nations of Persia and some of them under Roman sway, they bring in merchandise and carry on their dealings with each other there' (*History of the Wars,* II, XXV).

The transit trade declined during the years of Arab domination and the heavy taxes imposed by the Abbassid rulers ruined the country. Silver had virtually disappeared; those who could not pay their taxes were subjected to harsh treatment and many were driven to suicide. Conditions improved gradually when the Bagratids came to power. At that time Armenia constituted the neutral territory where Byzantium and the Caliphate, at war with one another, could carry on commercial exchanges. This international trade was the main source of revenue of such towns as Ani, Kars and Artsn near Theodosiopolis through which the highway from the Caliphate to Trebizond passed. Another route connected Ani and Kars with the important Georgian commercial centre of Ardanuch and proceeded from there to the eastern shores of the Black Sea. Artsn had been founded as an open city when the population of Theodosiopolis was transferred there, and it owed its great prosperity entirely to trade. It was in direct communication with Trebizond, and westward with Erzinjan and other towns within the Byzantine empire. The Armenian historian Aristakes of Lastivert, who witnessed the capture and pillage of the city by the Seljuks in 1049, also speaks of the great wealth accumulated by the inhabitants of Artsn. Usury increased with the spread of a monetary economy both at Artsn and in other cities.

With the Seljuk conquest Armenia lost for a while its important position in world trade. More favourable conditions existed in the thirteenth century at the time of Georgian suzerainty over the northern provinces of Armenia, and this period co-

incided with the establishment of commercial relations between
Venice and Genoa and the Black Sea ports. The creation of the
vast empire of the Mongols facilitated exchanges between the
Far East, Central Asia and the Caucasian lands. The northern
routes were used in preference to those farther south. One of
these northern highways passed through Caspian Turkestan to
the northern parts of the Black Sea, another crossed Armenia
on the way to Trebizond.

Numerous buildings erected in the thirteenth and early
fourteenth centuries in Armenia, as well as important donations
made to the monasteries, testify to the considerable monetary
wealth of the landed nobility and even more of the merchant
class. In the dedicatory inscription of the church of St Gregory
which he erected in 1215, Tigran Honents' lists the villages,
hostelries, private baths, mills and so forth which he donated.
One Sahmadin, the son of Avetik, reports that in 1261 he spent
40,000 gold ducats on building his summer palace at Mren.
Another wealthy merchant, by the name of Umek, had bought
the monastery of Getik for a like sum. It has been estimated
that a Venetian gold ducat was equivalent to 12 gold francs,
and this gives some idea of the vast wealth of some of these
merchants.

It is surprising that no Armenian coinage existed during the
prosperous Bagratid period; only coins struck by the kings of
Fig. 8 Lori are known. Byzantine and Arab currency were used for
the commercial transactions as well as for domestic use. In the
thirteenth century, at the time of the active maritime trade of
the Black Sea, Venetian gold coins circulated in Armenia, as
can be seen by the inscriptions mentioned above; no doubt
Georgian currency also changed hands there, as did of course
that of the Mongols in the late thirteenth century and the fourteenth century.

The transit trade was not the only source of wealth; Armenia
also exported raw materials from the mines, livestock, cereals

Fig. 8   Coin of Kiurike II, King of Lori in Armenia (after Lang)

and manufactured goods. Silver, copper, iron, arsenic, borax and salt figure among the exports mentioned in Arabic sources. Armenian horses and mules were highly prized; fish from Lake Van and from the river Arax were exported to Mesopotamia, Syria and Iran and fish, mules and falcons formed part of the tribute to the caliphate. The Arab geographers also mention the very large trees of the Armenian forests, in particular the walnut. According to at-Tabari, wheat was exported to Baghdad.

Armenia had a flourishing textile industry and its mineral and vegetable dyes were already known in Antiquity. In the Arab period the purple dye made from the kermes (see p. 12)— or *kirmiz*, as the Arabs called it—fetched a high price on the markets. Artaxata was the centre of the dye industry in Armenia and Baladhuri calls it Karya-al-Kirmiz, that is the Kirmiz village, because of the fame of its dye.

Armenian textiles and carpets also featured in the annual tribute. Ibn Khaldun includes in the tax-list 20 large carpets in relief in addition to the fish, mules and falcons mentioned above. Together with the land tax the Armenians sent to the Buwaihid sultan 30 large carpets in relief, 500 pieces of striped silk and 30 falcons. According to Ibn-Hawkal these carpets with a raised pattern had 'scarcely an equal in any place which possesses manufactures resembling them'. The ninth-century Arab writer

Djahiz considered that the best and most expensive draperies were the crimson ones made with Armenian goat hair, and he rated these higher than the striped silks and brocades of Sasanian and Byzantine manufacture. The Arab writers frequently refer to the trouser bands made in Armenia as having 'no equal in the world'. Armenian historians also refer to silk materials woven with gold and having figural representations. A veil on which are embroidered a tiger and a lion with silk and gold threads was discovered at Ani. A few silk textiles preserved in the bindings of manuscripts and the portraits of kings such as that of Gagik of Kars give us an idea of the range of the designs.

Plate 7

Plate 55

Armenia also exported furs and leather goods. Constantine Porphyrogenitus mentions the leather bath-tubs 'prepared in the Armenian fashion' which the Byzantine emperors took with them on their campaigns.

Trade was also basic to the economics of the Cilician king-dom. Cilicia was the starting point of one of the principal land routes to Tabriz and on to inner Asia. From Ayas (Lajazzo), this route crossed the Anti-Taurus range and proceeded by way of Sivas and Erzinjan along the valley of the river Arax and the shores of the Caspian Sea to Tabriz. Another route branched off at Erzinjan and followed the course of the Euphrates and the Tigris. The Mongol alliance facilitated the journeys of the many merchants and of travellers such as Marco Polo, who adopted the route which started in Cilicia. The port of Ayas thus became one of the principal emporiums of the Near East and after the capture of the Syrian and Palestinian sea ports by the Egyptians, one of the chief outlets to the Mediterranean for goods brought from Central Asia. 'For you must know,' wrote Marco Polo, 'that all the spicery and the cloths of silk and gold, and the other valuable wares that come from the interior are brought to that city, and the merchants of Venice and Genoa, and other countries, come hither to sell their goods and to buy what they lack.' Corycus, in western Cilicia, was another important port.

Tarsus was also a maritime city in the Middle Ages, the Cydnus having not yet been obstructed by sand; moreover, navigable waterways connected the towns of Adana and Mamistra with the sea.

By a treaty signed in March 1201, King Leo I (II) granted special privileges to the Genoese merchants; they were exempted from paying duties on their exports and imports, and they received permission to have commercial establishments in the capital, at Sis, as well as at Mamistra and Tarsus. Similar privileges were granted to the Venetians, by virtue of a treaty signed in December of the same year; with this difference, that only Mamistra is mentioned as the place assigned for their commercial establishments. In the course of the thirteenth and fourteenth centuries these treatises were renewed and the Italian merchants, in particular the Venetians, were granted additional privileges. Other foreign merchants whose ships visited Ayas and took part in the trading activities of this port included the Pisans, Florentines, Sicilians and the Catalans, and men from Montpellier and Marseilles.

Such charters and deeds, the detailed account of the commercial activities of Cilicia recorded by the Florentine Francesco di Balducci Pegolotti in his *Pratica della mercatura,* as well as some documents concerning damages, have enabled us to list many of the commodities that were imported and exported, and to envisage the vast scale of the international trade carried on in Cilicia. The Armenians exported a large amount of livestock—horses, mules, oxen, sheep and poultry; also buffalo hides, wool, cotton. Cloths made of goat hair were greatly prized because of its length and density. The forests on the slopes of the Taurus provided abundant timber for export. There were rich iron and salt mines. Wheat, wine, dry raisins and raw silk are also mentioned among the exports, but evidence is lacking concerning manufactured products. We do not know, for instance, whether the flourishing textile industry of Armenia also existed to any large extent in Cilicia. The sale of slaves was another important source of revenue; it was stipulated, however, that if these slaves happened to be Christians they were not to be sold to Muslims or to persons who were willing to sell them to Muslims.

Plate 6

Unlike those of Armenia, the rulers of Cilicia had their own coinage, and a few coins have been attributed to the period of the barony. Gold coins are rare, the bulk of Cilician coinage consisting of silver and copper coins. Broadly speaking, the following designs were most prevalent. To start with the obverse: this frequently shows the king enthroned, or on horseback, or sometimes it is only the king's head. On the few coronation coins of Leo I (II), he is represented kneeling before Christ. The obverse of one type of silver coin, issued by Het'um I, shows the king and queen facing one another and together holding a cross; the queen was included since she alone was of royal lineage and Het'um was, in actual fact, the prince consort. Among the designs on the reverse are found a cross between two lions rampant, a lion walking or holding a cross, a simple Greek cross, a cross with stars or with ornamental leaves at the base. On the reverse of the gold coins of Costandin II a castle with one turret or three is represented, while on his silver coins he stands holding a sword in his right hand and a cross in his left.

Wars and invasions had caused mass migrations of Armen, ians; with the development of international trading many of them travelled as merchants and settled in foreign countries. We know of several hostelries founded in different Italian towns during the thirteenth and fourteenth centuries; these were in part religious establishments but they also took in merchants and other travellers. Some men and even families went to more distant lands, even as far as China. In a letter written in 1318, the catholic bishop Peregrine reports that the Nestorians of China had not allowed other Christians to build churches in Khan,baliq, the seat of the great Khan. But, he goes on to say, when the archbishop John had arrived he had built several churches. 'And other nations of Christians who hate the schismatic Nestorians have followed Brother John, and specially the Armenians who are now building themselves a remarkable church which they mean to give him.' In this same letter there is reference to 'a good church with a residence' which a certain Armenian lady 'had built in the city of Zaitun'. The Franciscan missionary Andrew of Perugia also speaks of this 'sufficiently beautiful large church' built at Zaitun by this Armenian lady, which, 'after it had been made a cathedral by the Archbishop, she gave of her own will while she was living and left at death with adequate endowment to Brother Gerard the Bishop, who was the first to occupy the same see, and to our Brothers who are with him.' Zaitun (Ch'u'an-chou) was near the Treaty Port of Amoy in Fu-chien, and this 'wealthy lady' was no doubt a member of a family of merchants who had settled in China in favour of the alliance with the Mongols, and who had acquired wealth through the caravan trade which carried goods from China to Cilicia.

CHAPTER V

Religion

VERY little is known about the primitive religion of the Armenians. The lives of the eponymous and other legendary heroes contain elements which scholars have explained by other mythological tales. Thus Hayk, as the bowman who killed the tyrant Bel, has been compared to Apollo-Hekatebolos; his migrations recall those of Apollo-Helios and like him he is a cyclical divinity. The giant Turk, a descendant of Hayk, has been compared with the god of storms and thunder of the Hittite pantheon whom the Hurrians called Teshub. The myth of Attis and Cybele is reflected in the legend of Ara the Beautiful beloved by the Assyrian queen Semiramis.

During the historical period the Iranian divinities formed the Armenian pantheon. Ahura-Mazda, the father of all the gods, the creator of heaven and earth was worshipped under the name of Aramazd; he was 'the great and the powerful', 'dispenser of fertility on earth', 'author of all gifts', and his principal shrine was at Ani-Kamakh. Mithra, identified with the omnipotent sun, god of light and fire, protector of truth and justice, was known as Mihr. Anahita (Anahit), goddess of fertility, mother of all wisdom, became the favourite goddess and protector of the Armenians. Her feast was celebrated in spring and in autumn with many songs and dances, and several temples were dedicated to her. Of these the most famous was the temple of Erez, and because of her golden statue erected there she was known as the 'golden mother'. Verethragna, the god of war and victory, was worshipped under the name of Vahagn, and his principal shrine was at Ashtishat together with that of his paramour Astghik, the goddess of love. Tir, the scribe of Aramazd, was the god of science who recorded man's good and evil deeds; a school of diviners was connected with his temple, where various arts were taught and where dreams were interpreted. Barshamin and the goddess Nanē, probably of Syrian origin, also formed part of the Armenian pantheon.

In the History of the Conversion of Armenia, by Agathangelus, where the destruction of all the pagan temples is related, these divinities appear under the local Armenian forms of their Iranian names, but in the History of Moses of Khoren we find their Greek equivalents: Aramazd= Zeus; Mihr= Hephaestus; Anahit = Artemis; Vahagn = Heracles; Astghik = Aphrodite; Tir= Apollo, and Nanē= Athena; only Barshamin has retained the original form of his name. This is characteristic of the syncretism which took place in other areas of the Near East, ostensibly during the Hellenistic period, although the earlier names survived and occur more frequently in Armenian writings than their Greek equivalents. Evidence of similar syncretisms is to be found elsewhere. In the ruins of a Zoroastrian temple built at Persepolis, shortly after its destruction by Alexander, votive inscriptions in Greek designate Ahura-Mazda, Mithra and Anahita respectively as Zeus Megistos, Apollo and Athena. At Nimrud-Dagh, Antiochus I of Commagene is represented with the divinities Zeus-Oromasdes (Ahura-Mazda), Heracles-Verethragna and Apollo-Mithra.

The intrusion of Greek elements into a religion of Iranian origin also becomes apparent through Moses of Khoren's account of the cult statues that were brought from Greek cities and the Greek priests who came with them. Attributing to King Artashes what in reality concerns Tigran the Great, he writes that he brought from 'Asia' the gilt bronze statues of Artemis, Apollo and Heracles, the latter being the work of Scyllis and Dipoenus of Crete; the statues of the Olympian Zeus, of Artemis, Athena, Hephaestus and Aphrodite which he found in Greece he sent to Armenia. In a slightly later passage he speaks of the priests who had accompanied the statues.

It is difficult to ascertain how much of the specific information concerning these cult statues is correct, but the account, as a whole, cannot be rejected. The presence of Greek priests in Armenia has been confirmed by the discovery of the Greek inscription at Armavir. Scyllis and Dipoenus, the only sculptors mentioned by name, are known from other sources; they were born in Crete and were active in Argos and Sicyon around the middle of the sixth century BC. They are said to have founded an important school of sculpture in the Peloponnesus and Pliny actually mentions a statue of Heracles among their works.

Plate 5

Finally, the head of a bronze effigy of Artemis-Anahita, now at the British Museum, discovered at Erez (Erzinjan) is a Greek work.

Thus an Irano-Greek form of paganism prevailed and though officially paganism was abolished in the early fourth century, we know that in Armenia, as elsewhere, there remained for some time a considerable number of pagans, and ancient beliefs long survived in the native folklore and customs.

According to the Armenian tradition the Gospel was preached in Armenia by Thaddeus, one of the Seventy, in the southern part of the country, and by Bartholomew, the Apostle, in the north; they are therefore considered as the 'First Illuminators' of Armenia. The number of converts must have considerably increased in the course of the second and third centuries, for there were persecutions under King Artashes about AD 110, and under King Khosrov, about AD 230. The names of several martyrs of this early period are known through the Armenian martyrology. Tertullian includes Armenia among the countries whose people were present in Jerusalem on the day of Pentecost, an indication that in his time there were considerable numbers of Christians in Armenia. Eusebius quotes a letter written in AD 254 by the patriarch Dionysius of Alexandria to Meruzhan (Mitrozanes), bishop of Armenia.

Fresh persecutions started in AD 287, under King Trdat, and

it was during his reign that Christianity finally triumphed. It was proclaimed as state religion after Trdat's conversion by Saint Gregory, the 'Second Illuminator' of Armenia. Gregory, son of the Arsacid prince Anak, who had slain King Khosrov, had been reared in Caesarea in Cappodocia and brought up in the Christian religion. Having returned to Armenia, his identity was revealed to King Trdat, the son of Khosrov, who after torturing Gregory cast him into the pit of the dungeon of Artashat, where he miraculously survived for about fifteen years, being fed by a pious widow. Following the martyrdom of the maiden Hrip'simē, who had refused the advances of the king, and also those of her companions and of the abbess Gayanē who had led them to Vagharshapat, Trdat was afflicted by the state of insanity known as lycanthropy, in which he imagined himself to have been transformed into a wild boar—or as the story goes, in which he had assumed the shape of a wild boar. Urged by his sister who believed that only Gregory could heal him, Trdat ordered the latter's release from the pit. Whereafter Trdat was duly converted and healed. A mass conversion of the people took place at the same time. By an edict Christianity was proclaimed as the state religion. The traditional date for this event is AD 301, but recent investigations suggest that it was not before 314. However, this would still make Armenia the first country to have officially recognized Christianity, since Constantine's decree of 313 was only an edict of tolerance.

Gregory, who was a layman at the time, received episcopal consecration from Leontius, Archbishop of Caesarea, and he was chosen by Trdat and the people as the head of the Armenian Church. With pious zeal, Trdat and Gregory scoured the country destroying the temples and the statues of the pagan divinities and building churches in their place. A cathedral church was erected in the capital and the site was called Etchmiadzin, meaning where 'The Only-Begotten descended'. According to the account of Agathangelus, both the place and the plan of the church had been revealed to Gregory in a vision in which the shining figure of the Son of God, surrounded by the angelic host, had appeared before him, holding a golden hammer in His hand; four crosses of light also appeared, three of them marking the sites where the memorials to the three martyrs Hrip'simē, Gayianē and Marianē were to be erected, and the fourth, the tallest, that of the cathedral.

The early history of the established Church shows that in Armenia, as elsewhere, there were still many pagans and that among the Christians themselves there were dissenting sects. But the most serious threat, in particular in the eastern sections under Persian rule, was the repeated attempts made by the Sasanian kings to introduce Mazdaism. The heroic resistance offered by the Armenian people at the battle of Avarayr, already mentioned, is but one chapter in the story of their steadfast defence of their faith.

The invention of the Armenian alphabet in the early fifth century, discussed in the chapter devoted to Literature and Learning, strongly contributed towards strengthening the national character of the Church.

In the early sixth century the Armenian Church broke away. The extant creed was based on that of Nicaea, and the Church had fully accepted the decisions of the first three councils, those of Nicaea, Constantinople and Ephesus. Its doctrinal position was close to that of the Church of Alexandria, agreeing with the christological formula of 'one nature united in the Incarnate Word'. The writings of the fifth century show the growing opposition to any belief or definition which might tend to separate the human and divine natures in Christ. The Nestorians, who followed this belief, and who formed an important group on the southern borders of Armenia, protected as they were by the Persian rulers, appear to have attempted to introduce Nestorianism into Armenia during the second half of the fifth century. The strong opposition of the Armenians to Nestorianism to a certain extent governed their attitude toward the council of Chalcedon; for they considered that the formula adopted at this council, by too sharply distinguishing between the two natures, actually tended to separate them and was thus equivalent to the Nestorian heresy. Both condemnation of Nestorianism and repudiation of the Council of Chalcedon were pronounced at the Council which met at Dvin in AD 506. The list of heretics who were anathematized included Eutyches, showing that the Council also took a definite position against the Monophysite doctrine.

Both the Orthodox and the Roman Catholic Church have erroneously considered the Armenians as Monophysites. The Armenian Church has always violently rejected the mingling or the confusion of the two natures in Christ, and recognized in Him a divine and a human nature, a complete humanity animated by a rational soul. Adopting the Cyrillian definition of 'one nature united in the Incarnate Word', it has maintained that to speak of two natures after the union, as did the Chalce-donians, was to revert to the Nestorian heresy.

The doctrinal position taken by the Armenian Church and its repudiation of the Acts of the Council of Chalcedon, which by separating her from the other Churches was to a large measure instrumental in preserving its individuality, were at the same time at the root of many of the difficulties in its relations with Byzantium. For throughout the course of their mutual relations, the Byzantines employed every means—at times persuasion through discussions, but much more often intimidation, perse-cution and mass deportations—in order to bring the Armenians into the Orthodox fold. Similarly, during the period of the Cilician kingdom, the religious question loomed large in the relations with the West and above all with the Papacy.

If from the doctrinal problems and the relations with other Christian communities, we turn to the position of the Armenian Church within the nation, we can see that it was the principal source of national unity; the one organization that remained active when the country was overrun and occupied by the enemy, and political life was destroyed. Guardian of the language and of the secular traditions of the people, the Church was one of the principal strongholds of Armenian nationalism.

CHAPTER VI

Literature and Learning

A RMENIAN is an independent branch of the family of Indo-European languages, as independent for instance as Greek or Albanian; also like these two languages it has no descendants. According to the Greek historian Eudoxus the Armenians spoke a language very similar to Phrygian, but in the opinion of the majority of modern linguists, despite a number of coincidences between these two languages, they cannot be considered as closely related.

Because of the absence of early written documents one cannot follow the various stages of the development of Armenian during the centuries extending from the Indo-European period to the fifth century AD when the Armenian alphabet was invented. Some scholars believe that the pictograms engraved on rocks in the valley of the Arax may be a primitive form of the Armenian script, but such statements remain highly hypothetical since the pictograms have not been deciphered. The historian Moses of Khoren reports that there existed a pagan, temple literature in Armenia. He does not specify what type of script was used, but in another context he refers to Armenian secular works written with Persian or Greek letters. There is no material evidence to corroborate these statements, the old inscriptions found so far in Armenia being either in Greek or Aramaic; a few later ones are in Latin.

By the time Armenian came to be written it had become a highly developed language, with a wide and precise vocabulary and an exact grammar. Some of the modifications of the Indo-European phonic system and grammatical forms that can then be observed were caused by the influence of the Urartian language, and that of other groups with whom the Armenians came into contact after their establishment in their new homeland. For instance, although Armenian has retained almost all the cases of the Indo-European declension, it has lost the distinction between genders. During the centuries of Iranian domination and especially when the Arsacid dynasty, of Parthian origin, ruled in Armenia, many Iranian words were introduced into the Armenian vocabulary. Iranian suffixes were used to coin new words, and even some locutions are patterned on Iranian ones. But Iranian had virtually no influence on the grammar.

Greek and Syriac words, far less numerous than the Parthian, were primarily introduced into the Armenian vocabulary after the establishment of Christianity, although Greek influence had already penetrated into Armenia in the Seleucid period. At the time of Tigran the Great and his successors Greek was spoken by many members of the aristocracy. Famous Greek men had sought refuge at Tigranocerta. Plutarch mentions the Athenian orator Amphicrates, and Metrodorus of Scepsis, 'an eloquent and learned man, and so close an intimate as commonly to be called the king's father'. Greek plays were performed at the theatre of Tigranocerta and at Artashat. At the marriage of the son of the Parthian king with the sister of King Artavasd (son of Tigran the Great) there were great festivities, and Greek compositions suitable to the occasion were recited before the royal couple.

These events are related by Plutarch in his life of Crassus. A scene from *The Bacchae* of Euripides was being performed by the actor Jason when the head of Crassus was brought in and thrown into the midst of the company. Whereupon Jason seized the head and, acting the part of a frenzied bacchante, sang, to the great delight of the audience, the lyric passage

> *We've hunted down a mighty chase today,*
> *And from the mountain bring the noble prey.*
> trans. Dryden

For the Parthians, adds Plutarch, were not ignorant of the Greek language and Artavasdes was so expert in it, that he had written tragedies, orations and histories, some of which were still extant. Another learned Armenian of this period, whose name has come down to us, was called Tiran. Taken to Rome as a prisoner by Lucullus, he became a close friend of Cicero's, achieved renown as an orator and a grammarian, and founded a library. Greek learning continued to be honoured during the ensuing centuries. In Athens there were Armenians among the fellow-students of Gregory of Nazianzus and Basil of Caesarea. One of their teachers, for whom Gregory later composed an epitaph, was the Armenian Proheresius, whom Sozomenus calls 'the most celebrated sophist of the age'. According to his pupil and biographer, Eunapius, Proheresius 'came from that part of Armenia which borders most on Persia'; he had gone to Antioch as a youth, and later to Athens. Eunapius gives a detailed account of his master's successful career in Athens; he describes his visit to the Gallic provinces, on the invitation of Emperor Constans, who later sent him to Rome to display his eloquence. The Romans, writes Eunapius, 'made and set up in his honour a bronze statue, life-size, with the inscription: Rome, the Queen of cities, to the King of eloquence'. According to Libanius a statue had also been erected in Athens in honour of Proheresius.

Libanius himself numbered Armenians among his students in Antioch. In one of his letters he writes that not a few of his students are to be found in the cities of Galatia and as many in Armenia. In his book on the Students of Libanius, based on the latter's correspondence, P. Petit has recorded the names of twenty Armenian students; some of these were Christians, like the sophist Proheresius, others were still pagans. The Armenians formed the most important contingent of students from the eastern provinces of the empire. There had also been Armenians among the fellow-students of Libanius; one, Leontius, became

81

a professor in Armenia and he sent some of his pupils to Antioch for further study with Libanius. Leontius was later appointed governor of Palestine and then of Galatia by the emperor Julian. Several of Libanius's Armenian students were also given important positions in the Byzantine government, positions for which their thorough training in Greek had qualified them. In the fourth century Syrian learning had become as important as Greek, especially in the eastern part of the country and many Armenians went to study at Edessa and Nisibis.

But if there were no written texts before the invention of the Armenian alphabet, there was an oral transmission. Fragments of poems have been preserved, primarily by Moses of Khoren. One of these refers to the birth of the god Vahagn.

> *Heaven and earth were in travail*
> *And was in travail the crimson sea*
> *And in the sea the red reed was in travail.*
> *From the mouth of the reed issued smoke*
> *From the mouth of the reed issued flame*
> *And in the flame ran a young child.*
> *His hair was of fire*
> *Of flame was his beard*
> *And his eyes were suns.*

Other poems, known as Songs of Koght'en, are parts of epic poems celebrating the deeds of kings such as Artashes and his son Artavazd. While Artashes was building the city of Artashat, the Alans invaded his kingdom. Artashes marched against them, drove them beyond the Kura and took prisoner the king's son. The Alan king sought peace, promising to give in return for his son whatever Artashes desired. Artashes refused, where-upon the king's daughter Sat'enik came to the bank of the river and, through an interpreter, spoke as follows:

'I speak to thee, o brave Artashes
Who hast vanquished the brave nation of the Alans
Come, hearken to the request of the bright-eyed daughter of the Alans
Return the youth.
For it is not the custom of heroes, in revenge
To take the lives of the sons of other heroes
Or by making them prisoners to keep them as slaves
And establish eternal enmity
Between the men of two brave nations.'

Hearing the wise words of the princess, and captivated by her beauty, Artashes sent a messenger to the king of the Alans, asking his daughter in marriage. The king said:

'And whence can the brave Artashes give
Thousands after thousands and ten thousands upon ten thousands
In return for this virgin, the noble daughter of the Alans.'
The brave King Artashes mounted his fine black steed
And removing his red leathern cord (adorned) with golden rings
Like a swift-winged eagle he crossed the river
He cast the gold-ringed red cord
Around the waist of the maiden of the Alans
Causing much pain to the waist of the tender maiden
And swiftly bore her back to his camp.

And at their wedding feast the people sang:

Showers of gold rained when Artashes became a bridegroom
Pearls showered when Sat'enik became a bride.

Some of these songs were passed on by word of mouth until the eleventh century, for Gregory Magistros quotes a fragment referring to the death of Artashes which he had heard from some peasants.

It was through this oral literature, of which only scattered fragments have survived, that the Armenian language developed and reached such a high degree that the works of the fifth century constitute the golden age of Armenian literature.

The written literature starts with the invention of the Armenian alphabet which most scholars date to AD 406. After the establishment of the Christian religion in Armenia, the liturgy was performed in Greek or in Syriac, according to the region, and the lessons from the Scriptures were orally translated into Armenian by a group of trained priests. Since it did not cater for the spiritual needs of the people such a state of affairs could not go on indefinitely. There were, however, other circumstances which made it even more imperative, in the early fifth century, to make of Armenian a written language. Mazdaist propaganda had become more intensive, and effective measures had to be taken against it. An Armenian literature, developing by means of an Armenian script, could best serve the needs of the Church both where the edification of the people was concerned and as a barrier to the dissemination of Mazdaist literature.

The Catholicos Sahak and King Vramshapuh, fully aware of the situation, entrusted the task of inventing an alphabet to the learned cleric MesropMashtots', who was well versed in Greek and Syriac languages. There already existed some Armenian letters invented by a Syrian bishop named Daniel, but these were not well adapted to the language and had not been used. Mesrop had therefore to start anew. A journey of study and consultation took him and his students first to Amida, then to Edessa and Samosata. In the latter city he met the calligrapher Rufinus who helped him to give final shape to the characters. When Mesrop returned to Armenia, he brought with him an alphabet, composed of thirtysix letters, a remarkable phonetic instrument, exactly corresponding to all the variations

Ա ա	a	Կ կ	k[g]	Ռ ռ	rh		
Բ բ	b[p]	Հ հ	h	Ս ս	s		
Գ գ	g[k]	Ձ ձ	dz[ts]	Վ վ	v		
Դ դ	d[t]	Ղ ղ	gh	Տ տ	t[d]		
Ե ե	e¹	Ճ ճ	ch[j]	Ր ր	r		
Զ զ	z	Մ մ	m	Ց ց	ts'		
Է է	ē	Յ յ	y²	Ւ ւ	w		
Ը ը	ě	Ն ն	n	Փ փ	p'		
Թ թ	t'	Շ շ	sh	Ք ք	k'		
Ժ ժ	zh	Ո ո	o	Օ օ	ō		
Ի ի	i	Չ չ	ch'	Ֆ ֆ	f		
Լ լ	l	Պ պ	p[b]				
Խ խ	kh	Ջ ջ	j[ch]				
Ծ ծ	ts[dz]						

Fig. 9   The Armenian alphabet

of the phones of the Armenian language. The designs of 22 out
of the 36 letters were based on Greek letters, while Syriac letters
served as models for some of the others; but in each case modifications were introduced in order to give the script some degree
of unity. After the Armenian alphabet Mesrop also devised one
for the Georgians and another for the Caucasian Albanians.

A great task lay ahead: to translate the Scriptures, the liturgy,
the important writings of Greek and Syrian Church Fathers,
and to train scholars who could undertake this work. Mesrop

Fig. 9

sent his students for further study of Syriac and Greek to Edessa, Caesarea, and Constantinople, with instructions to bring back choice manuscripts, and he founded several schools in Armenia. The first was that of Vagharshapat, the see of the Catholicos; schools were also established in the monastic centres of the eastern part of Armenia which was still under the control of King Vramshapuh. In the western part, under Byzantine domination, where no Armenian ruler had been appointed after the death of the last king, the establishment of schools presented greater difficulties, but after a visit by Mesrop to the Emperor Theodosius and to the Patriarch Atticus the necessary permission was obtained.

As was natural, the first work to be undertaken was the translation of the Bible. A Syriac original was used, but the translation having been deemed unsatisfactory, the Bible was translated again from the Greek text of the Septuagint sent from Constantinople. This translation was revised by the Catholicos Sahak himself who was an excellent Greek scholar. Through its faithfulness to the original and the elegance of its style the Armenian translation ranks high among the different versions of the Bible. The different books of the liturgy were next prepared, for the use of the Church.

Many are the translations from Syriac and Greek, made principally in the course of the two centuries after the invention of the alphabet. Two general observations should be made in regard to these. In the first place these translations have in several instances preserved texts of the Greek and Syriac ecclesiastical writers the originals of which are lost; they have thus contributed to the general knowledge of the literature of this early period. Such works include the first part of the *Chronicle* of Eusebius, the well-known ecclesiastical historian of the fourth century; the *Commentaries on the Benediction of Moses* by Hippolytus; and the *Refutation of the Definition of the Council of Chalcedon* by Timothy Aelurus, Patriarch of Alexandria. Until 1957, when sections of Ephraim's *Commentary on the Diatessaron* were discovered in the original Syriac, this important work was only known through the Armenian version; even after this discovery the latter has retained its significance since the Syriac text is incomplete.

The second observation concerns the choice of texts, their wide range being indicative of the varied interests of the Armenian educated classes. In addition to the writings of the Greek and Syrian Church Fathers, the translations comprise secular works like the *Alexander Romance* by Pseudo-Callisthenes, the *Grammar* of Dionysius Thrax, treatises of Philo Judaeus and numerous philosophical writings, in particular those of the Neo-Platonic philosophers such as Porphyry, Probus, Diodochus, Olympiodorus the Younger and others. Aristotle, more than any other ancient philosopher, exercised a great influence on Armenian thought; the translations comprise the *Categories, Metaphysics, Analytics,* the *De Interpretatione* and several minor works. The continued interest in Aristotle can be judged from the commentaries written by medieval Armenian authors, as well as from the large number of the copies of Aristotle's works made throughout the centuries. At the Library of Erevan alone, the *Matenadaran,* there are almost three hundred manuscripts of Aristotle's works.

Literary activity was not limited to translations; original religious and historical works were composed as well as hagiographic texts, homilies and hymns. The treatise *Against the Sects,* written by Eznik of Koghb who belonged to the first group of translators and pupils of Mesrop-Mashtots', is a refutation of Zoroastrianism, Gnosticism, Manichaeism and the heresy of Marcion. Father L. Mariès has regarded it rather as a treatise on God and has therefore given the title *De Deo* to his edition and translation of this important text. The early historians were primarily interested in contemporary events. Agathangelus (obviously an assumed name), who claims to have been a secretary of King Trdat, wrote the *History of the Conversion of Armenia by Gregory the Illuminator,* a work which in spite of its weaknesses is important for the early religious and political history of Armenia. One of the early group of translators, Koriun, wrote the biography of his master Mesrop-Mashtots'. *The History of Vardan and the Battle of the Armenians,* composed by Eghishē, covers the period from 430 to 465, and has as its main section an epic account of the battle of Avarayr and the struggle against Mazdaism. The same events are also recounted by Ghazar P'arpets'i (Lazarus of P'arpi), whose *History* however runs from 384 to 485. Moses of Khoren (Movses Khorenats'i), whose name has frequently appeared in the preceding pages, had a more ambitious aim, for his *History,* though confined to the period before 440, begins with the origins of the Armenians. The author, a putative nephew of Mesrop-Mashtots', says he composed it at the request of prince Sahak Bagratuni, but the fifth-century date of his work, traditionally accepted and maintained by some critics, has been seriously questioned by others who consider that it cannot have been composed before the eighth, or even according to some, before the early ninth century. Written in an elegant and poetic style, this *History,* despite its inaccuracies, especially in the chronology, is rich in information of all kinds on the early centuries.

Historiography continued to occupy a foremost place in the literary production of the following centuries. Some of these historical works, although limited in their scope, are significant because their authors deal with more or less contemporary events. Thus the *History of Heraclius,* attributed to Sebeos, describes in detail the Arab invasions of Persia, Armenia and the Byzantine empire down to the year AD 661. The priest Ghevond gives an equally detailed account of the Arab conquest and occupation of Armenia, from 661 to 788. Aristakes of Laztivert witnessed the Seljuk conquest and his *History* is a valuable source for Byzantine as well as for Armenian history. Aristakes was one of several historians who flourished in the tenth and eleventh centuries. It became the fashion then to write so-called Universal Histories which began with the story of the Creation. The early sections are obviously devoid of historical value, even those which pertain to ancient Armenian history, for they are, by and large, summaries of the writings of the older historians. In a few cases, however, they have transmitted information from works which have since been lost, such as the *History* of Shapuh Bagratuni. The valuable parts are those which relate to the Bagratid period, and these acquire additional importance when the author happens to have taken an active part in the affairs of the realm, like the Catholicos John V. The chapters of his *History* in which John relates, for instance, his embassy to the Emir Yusuf and his imprisonment, give us first-hand information. He has also included in his work his correspondence with the Patriarch of Constantinople, Nicholas Mysticus. These are important documents concerning Armeno-Byzantine relations. Stephen of Taron, surnamed Asoghik, carried his *History* to the year 1004. He is a careful historian; his chronology is more accurate than is often the case, and he has taken the trouble to cite his sources. Both these authors dwell primarily on the history of the Bagratid rulers. A contemporary of theirs, Thomas Artsruni, concentrated his attention on the rulers of the province of Vaspurakan, to whom he himself was related. King Gagik is his hero, and he takes pride in describing the palace and the churches this ruler had erected. But Thomas also assembled all the available information on the early history of the Artsrunis and of the province of Vaspurakan. He relates how he travelled far and wide in order to collect his material, incidentally providing interesting information concerning customs of the inhabitants of the mountainous regions. By its general tenor, this *History of the Artsrunis* is comparable to the *History of the Family and the Province of Siunik'* written at the end of the thirteenth century by Stephen Orbelian, Bishop of Siunik' and also a scion of the

ruling family. Stephen had at his disposal the historical documents preserved at the monastery of Tat'ev, which he often cites
verbatim, and he also made wide use of the rich epigraphical
material provided by the inscriptions carved on the churches
and monasteries.

Because of the geographical position of Armenia her history
is in many respects part of the general history of the Near East,
and the information given by the Armenian writers often
concerns the history of the neighbouring nations. The most
important work in this respect is the *History of the Albanians* by
Movses Draskhurants'i, the only existing source on this Cauca-
sion nation. The second book of the *History* of Ukhtanes is
devoted to the secession of the Georgians from the Armenian
Church in the sixth century; in it Ukhtanes dwells at some
length on the origin of the Georgians, on their history and on
the ethnology of the different tribes. The *History of the Nation
of the Archers* (that is the Mongols) by Grigor Akants', the
works of the thirteenth-century historians Vardan and Kirakos,
and the *Flor des Estoires de la Terre d'Orient* by Hayton (Het'um)
contain important data on the history, the customs and even
the language of the Mongols. Similarly the *Histories* of Matthew
of Edessa and of the Constable Smbat have some bearing on the
history of the Seljuks of Iconium and on the Crusades. Thus the
contribution made by the medieval Armenian historians
transcends the limits of their national history.

History apart, the literary works of this period consist almost
entirely of religious writings such as hagiographies, homilies and
commentaries on the Scriptures or on the liturgy. The collections
of Proverbs, with their moralizing tendency, had the similar aim
of edification. However, they throw—one might say, almost
unwillingly—much light on the customs of the time, and on
the injustices of the social order. With rare exceptions, the
poetry itself has a religious character. Pride of place belongs to
the *Book of Prayers* written in 1002 by the elegiac poet Grigor of

Narek. Each of the ninety-five poems grouped in this work begins with the words 'From the depth of the heart a soliloquy with God', and it gives expression to the mystical meditations of a deeply religious and fervent man, endowed with rare poetic gifts. Mysticism with poetic undertones also colours the prose writings of Gregory of Narek, for instance his *Panegyrics,* his *Commentary on the Canticle of Canticles,* or the *History of the Cross of Aparank'* in which he describes the arrival from Constantinople in the year 983 of a fragment of the True Cross. The hymns and longer poems composed in the eleventh century by the Catholicos Nerses the Gracious reveal a more serene though equally devout nature. His elegy on the Fall of Edessa shows how deeply this disaster affected the Armenians of Cilicia. In the first part of this poem, Edessa personified calls on the sees of the five ancient patriarchates—Jerusalem, Rome, Constantinople, Alexandria and Antioch—to lament her fate. She then turns to Armenia, and in a long excursus the poet describes the past glories of the kingdom, contrasting them with its sad, present state. In the same manner the beauties of the city of Edessa, her glory and her riches, are recalled, followed by a long description of the siege and capture. Incidentally, it provides the most detailed account of this war to have come down to us. The poem ends with the prediction that the Franks will return to save the Christians. The *Elegy on the Fall of Jerusalem,* composed on the same pattern by the younger brother of Nerses, the Catholicos Grigor Dgha, is poetically less accomplished.

The layman Frik is an exception among the poets of this period. He lived at the time of the Mongol invasion of Great Armenia and his poems, written in the vulgar and not classical language, echo the sufferings of the people by the cruel wars. He inveighs alike against the exactions and tyranny of the feudal lords and the members of the higher clergy, and all forms of social inequality. Very little is known about his life, beyond what can be gleaned from his poems; but he was a man of the people and as such, their interpreter. Other laymen, bards and singers, composed poems, many of which are scattered in manuscripts and have not yet been seriously studied. Their publication would serve to present a more accurate image of medieval society in Armenia than do the religious poems. Some aspects of this may be seen in the tales grouped under the name of David of Sasun, which were preserved orally until collected and set down in several variants in the late nineteenth century. The first two cycles present successive generations of heroes of the province of Sasun. The last two centre around David, the young hero of fabulous strength who killed the tyrant Mesramelik' and liberated his country, while also referring to his son Mher. A national epic, its action takes place in the mountainous region of Sasun, south-west of Lake Van. It contains elements going back to early legends, while the sections which have an historical core refer to the time of Arab domina-tion in Armenia in the eighth–ninth centuries AD. There are many points of resemblance between it and the Byzantine epic of Digenis Akritas, though the two are independent, for it came into being at approximately the same period and in a similar border region.

We must now turn from the literary scene, and examine briefly the state of scientific learning in medieval Armenia. Whilst the Armenian commentaries on the works of Aristotle naturally throw light on certain of its aspects, it is more impor-tant to call attention to those whose original works contributed to the advancement of scientific knowledge in their country. The earliest among these men is the seventh-century scientist Ananias of Shirak. He himself, in a short autobiography, sets down the principal facts relating to his training and tells of his aspirations. He was born in the village of Anania, in the canton of Shirak, and at an early age set about learning philosophy. 'Being in great need', he writes, 'of the science of numbers, which I considered as the mother of all knowledge, I thought that there existed no harmony without numbers.' Finding no master in Armenia, Ananias went to Trebizond where, he was told, he would find the great teacher Tychikos, whose fame attracted students even from Constantinople. Ananias was very well received by Tychikos; he remained with him for eight years and acquired a thorough knowledge of mathematics, as well as some elements of other sciences. He read all the books in his teacher's library that had not been translated into Armenian; secular, scientific, historical and medical books, and those dealing with chronology. His own scientific works, written after his return to Armenia, comprise books on arithmetic, cosmography, the lunar cycle, chronology, weights and measures, and geography. The world, Ananias opined, was similar to an egg, having at its centre the Earth, like the yolk; around the Earth lay the air, like the white of the egg; and surrounding both, the sky. Contrary to the current view that the ocean encircled the Earth, he maintained that the waters were contained by the lands.

Of the various treatises by Ananias, one is of lasting importance, namely the *Geography*, hitherto attributed to Moses of Khoren. The general descriptions of the three continents, Europe, Africa and Asia, based to a large extent on the *Geography* of Ptolemy and even more on that of Pappus of Alexandria, do not add much to general knowledge, but the more detailed description of Armenia and its neighbouring countries, namely Georgia, Caucasian Albania, Persia and Mesopotamia, provide a wealth of information not to be found in earlier treatises. To fill out the picture, we have Anania's *Itinerary*, where the principal trade routes are indicated together with the distances between the important cities, and his treatise on *Weights and Measures* which includes a mixed table of Byzantine and Persian weights.

Scientific studies, which had been suspended during the centuries of Arab occupation, were resumed during the Bagratid period. One of the principal movers in this field was Gregory Pahlavuni, lord of Bjni, better known by his Byzantine title of Gregory Magistros. In a letter addressed to the Catholicos Petros he enjoins him to read the works of Ananias, which had been sadly neglected, and he asks for the loan of some of the manuscripts which contain important data on the exact sciences and music. Because of his marked interest in mathematics Gregory translated the *Elements* of Euclid, a translation made directly from the Greek original and not through the inter-mediary of a Syriac text, as was the case with the Arab version. Equally interested in philosophy, he translated two of the dialogues of Plato, the *Timaeus* and the *Phaedo*, and he was familiar with the works of the other Greek philosophers. Writing to two of his students who at the time were at the see of the Catholicos Petros I, mentioned above, he tells them that he has heard that the latter had given them the works of Aristotle; 'if', he adds, 'this is the collection in which Aristotle speaks of the celestial bodies and of the sphericity of the world, please send it to me, but if it is Porphyry's Introduction to the Cate-gories I need not ask you to send it, for I have known it ever since my early youth.'

Among the other Armenians whose works are connected with the exact sciences, the most important is John the Deacon (Hohannes Sarkavag) whom his contemporaries called a sophist or a philosopher. Author of a number of studies on philosophical as well as mathematical subjects, including a valuable treatise on polygonal numbers, he also introduced a reform of the Armenian calendar.

The life of John the Deacon and information gleaned from the correspondence of Gregory Magistros throw some light on the schools and teaching in medieval Armenia. In the seventh century Ananias of Shirak was, as we have seen, obliged to go to Trebizond in order to find a teacher; in the second half of the tenth century John the Deacon received his education at the monastery of Haghbat where he found not only masters who could train him but also in its large library copies of the ancient scientific and philosophical works. Having completed his studies, he went to Ani and founded there a school whose fame attracted students from all over of Armenia. Unfortunately we have few particulars about this school which appears to have been the first establishment of higher learning connected with a monastic establishment. Among the subjects that were taught there, the following are mentioned: grammar, with special reference to the work of Dionysius Thrax; philosophy, and in particular the works of Aristotle; mathematics, chronology, rhetoric as well as, naturally, theology. Somewhat earlier Gregory Magistros had also trained students, though it is not clear whether there was a regular school at Bjni or, as seems more probable, young men came to read under his guidance and benefit from his vast knowledge in the most diversified fields. The course of studies he outlines for his students in one of his letters is as follows: one must begin with the Scriptures followed by the study of mythology and old legends; next read excerpts from Homer, Plato and other ancient writers, and study arithmetic, music, geometry and astronomy. When these subjects have been mastered, one can pass to the higher realm of grammar, rhetoric and philosophy. As can be seen, this plan roughly corresponds to the medieval quadrivium and trivium, but we do not know to what extent it was put into execution and whether, for instance, it was followed in the school founded by John the Deacon.

The monasteries were the principal intellectual centres, the most ancient being the foundation known as the Seminary of Siunik'. One may question the accuracy of the thirteenth-century historian Stephen Orbelian when he states that to it alone the Catholicos Sahak and Mesrop-Mashtots' granted the privilege of translating the Bible and of writing commentaries of the Scriptures. Nevertheless, noted scholars did belong to this

Seminary, among them the sixth-century Bishop of Siunik', Peter, a philosopher and Hellenist of repute, and in the early eighth century, Bishop Stephen, who translated the writings of Dionysius the Areopagite and of Gregory of Nyssa, besides being the author of homilies, commentaries, and an explanation of the Grammar. After attending the Seminary of Siunik' he had pursued his studies in Athens and in Constantinople and had brought back with him several Greek manuscripts. Of the monastery of Tat'ev, also in the province of Siunik', later prominent, Stephen Orbelian wrote: 'It shone like the sun in the midst of the stars. It was renowned among all not only because of its buildings, but also because of its priests and monks who numbered about five hundred. It was filled with philosophers, profound as the sea . . . . ., its college was rich in scholars and doctors, skilful painters, incomparable scribes.' In the large monastic complexes, a separate building was erected to house the manuscripts. The library of the monastery of Haghbat was particularly rich and it is said that whenever a given work proved to be lacking, the monks made a special effort to find a model, to copy it and add it to their collection. In the late thirteenth and early fourteenth centuries the school of the monastery of Gladzor attracted students from the different provinces of Great Armenia and also from Cilicia. At the time of the Dominican missions, which made a number of converts among the lay population and even the monks, the abbot and the *Vardapets* of Gladzor were the staunch defenders of the national Church. Important monastic centres also flourished in Cilicia, and materially contributed towards maintaining connections with the mother country; their role in the national life can be summed up by quoting the words of the Catholicos Nerses the Gracious: 'The monasteries have been the pillars of the country, the fortresses against the enemy, and shining stars.'

CHAPTER VII

Architecture

ARMENIAN monuments were first brought to the attention of European scholars by French and English travellers of the nineteenth century. On the basis of their descriptions, drawings and plans, Auguste Choisy attempted the first critical study of Armenian architecture in his *Histoire de l'Architecture,* published in 1899. While considering this architecture as a provincial expression of Byzantine art, Choisy nevertheless pointed to certain specific forms and methods of construction, as well as to a possible Armenian influence on the monuments of the Balkans, in particular on those of Serbia. The relationship between Armenian and Byzantine architecture was studied in 1916 by G. Millet, in his book on *L'Ecole grecque dans l'architecture byzantine.* By that time a larger number of monuments had come to be known through the excavations carried out at Ani and other sites in Armenia, the expeditions of Russian archaeologists and the studies of Armenian scholars, especially those of the architect Th. Thoramanian. These studies were extensively used by J. Strzygowski in his monumental work *Die Baukunst der Armenier und Europa,* which appeared in 1918. From then on, Armenian monuments have been included in all general works devoted to medieval architecture and the many studies made by Armenian and foreign scholars in the course of the last forty years have greatly broadened the field of investigations.

Strzygowski claimed for Armenia a major role in the origins and development of Christian architecture. According to him the Armenians were the first to translate into stone the dome on squinches used in the brick architecture of northern Iran, and the first to design a church in the form of a square with small apse-like niches and crowned with a cupola. Strzygowski also maintained that the Armenians originated other types of domed buildings and he traced their influence in the art not only of Byzantium and other Christian countries of the Middle East but also of Western Europe, both in the Middle Ages and during the Renaissance. 'Greek genius at St Sophia and Italian genius at St Peter's', wrote Strzygowski, 'only realized more fully what the Armenians had originated.'

Though recognizing the great merit of Strzygowski's book—the first detailed investigation of Armenian architecture—most scholars have rejected the extreme claims he made. Excavation work in several different countries has increased the number of Early Christian monuments available for study and scholars have become aware, even more keenly than before, of the existence of similar types of contemporary buildings, far removed from one another. The studies of A. Grabar on the *martyria* (memorial chapels for Christian martyrs) and their relationship to the mausolea of late antiquity have put the entire problem of the origins and development of Christian architecture on a much broader basis. No one country can be considered as the fountain-head from which all others received their inspiration.

An opposite view has been recently put forward by G. Tchubinashvili. By arbitrarily post-dating, often by several centuries, the Armenian monuments, this scholar has sought to prove the priority and the superiority of the Georgian examples, thereby implying that the Armenian churches are but poor imitations of Georgian prototypes. Such statements, which disregard all the historical data, are unacceptable and have been rejected by other authorities. In fact there was a parallel development in both countries, especially during the early centuries when the Armenian and Georgian Churches were united, and contacts between them were close and frequent. There were, no doubt, mutual exchanges: Armenian and Georgian architects must have collaborated more than once, as can be seen from the Armenian inscriptions on the Georgian churches of Djvari and Ateni-Sion. The latter mentions the name of the architect

T'odosak and those of his assistants. Not by setting the architec/ tural monuments of the two countries in opposition but by considering them together will further light be thrown on a number of outstanding problems.

The monuments of Garni are the only vestiges of the pagan architecture of Armenia known to us. The excavations carried out there in recent years have brought to light the walls of the powerful fortifications and fourteen rectangular towers, a large vaulted hall and several smaller rooms of the royal palace, as well as part of the bath built to the north of the palace, consisting of four rooms with apsidal ends. The most important ruins are *Fig. 10* those of the temple built during the reign of Trdat I, shortly after AD 66, and which had survived until it was destroyed by *Plate 8* an earthquake in 1679. Now only the podium reached by nine steps, the lower courses of the walls of the naos and the pronaos, parts of the 24 Ionic columns and of the entablature remain. This type of Roman, peripteral temple is known through monuments in Asia Minor, such as the temples of Sagalas and Termes in Pisidia.

Several centuries separate the temple of Garni from the Christian edifices, of which the earliest extant examples do not

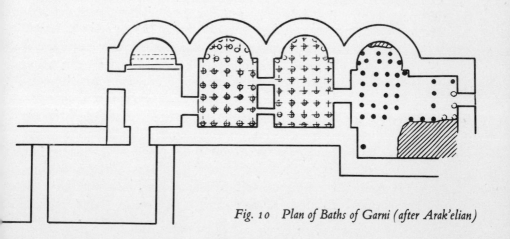

Fig. 10   Plan of Baths of Garni (after Arak'elian)

ante-date the late fifth century. And until other monuments are excavated we cannot trace the early stages of the development of Christian architecture in Armenia. But the period which extends from the late fifth to the middle of the seventh century witnessed a remarkable flowering to which many monuments testify. If at first sight it seems surprising that there should have been such an extensive building activity during these years when Armenia had lost her independence and the country was divided between Byzantium and Persia, we have only to recall what was said earlier about the position of the *nakharars,* and the wealth controlled both by them and by the Church, in order to see how it came about. The founders of the buildings whose names are recorded in the dedicatory inscriptions or by historians, are the Catholicoses, and the heads of the principal feudal families such as the Amatunis, the Mamikonians, the Kamsarakans and the Saharunis. The feudal organization thus favoured the proliferation of churches in different parts of the country. The absence of a centralized power which might have restricted church architecture to certain types, also partly explains the wide variety of design encountered during this period.

Armenian churches are built in the native volcanic stone which has a yellow, ochre, or even darker tint. For the walls a core of masonry rubble is lined on either side with thin, carefully cut and polished slabs; only the corner blocks are monolithic. This method of construction is used for the heavy piers as well as for the vaults. The churches, often small in size, nevertheless give the impression of solid strength. The inner articulations of the design are not always reflected in the uniform surfaces of the

Fig. 11   exterior. A rectangular contour may mask circular, polygonal or more complex forms, and only the triangular recesses of the outer walls will sometimes mark the points of juncture of the diverse elements. On occasion carved decorations and blind arcades all around the walls help to alleviate the austere aspect of the façades. The walls are pierced by a relatively small number of

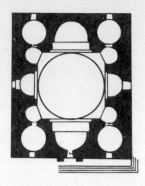

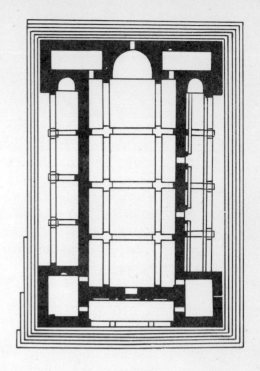

*Figs. 11, 12 Above, church of Avan,
erected by Catholicos John, 590–611;
right, Basilica of Ereruk, fifth-sixth
century (after Khatchatrian) 1 : 500*

windows. From the seventh century on, when domed structures
became the general rule, the pyramidal or conical roof covering
the dome on its high drum is a characteristic feature of the outer
aspect of Armenian churches. In building the domes over a
square or octagonal structure, the Armenian architects usually
resorted to the squinch, a small arch or half-conical niche at
the corners which allows the transition from the square to the
octagon, and from the octagon to a polygonal base for the drum
of the dome. Where the dome was supported by free-standing
pillars, they used pendentives—inverted, spherical triangles
placed between adjacent arches to form a continuous base for
the drum.

The earliest extant churches of Armenia are all basilicas, a
plan ultimately derived, as elsewhere in the Christian world,
from the halls of pagan public buildings. The Armenian

basilicas, whether aisleless or with three aisles, are always vaulted. They have no transept and nothing interrupts the unity of the interior space. Transverse arches, often of horseshoe profile, rest on the T-shaped piers and strengthen the vaults of nave and side aisles. A single roof sometimes covers all three aisles as at K'asakh, one of the earliest basilicas. In other churches the central nave rises higher than the aisles and is roofed separately. The basilica at Ereruk' and those originally planned for Tekor and Dvin, being larger, had lateral porches added, ending in small apses. The church of Ereruk' had a twin-towered façade, the only Armenian example of a design used in several Syrian churches, but these towers project laterally as in the Anatolian edifices.

Fig. 12

The basilican church did not remain in favour for long. From the late sixth century onwards it gave place to a wide variety of central, domed types. The remote origin of these central plans is to be sought in the heroa and mausolea of late antiquity and in the Early Christian *martyria,* but their sudden appearance in Armenia and the diversity of the plans suggest that various schemes had been tried out locally prior to the sixth century. This has been confirmed by the excavations recently undertaken under the cathedral of Etchmiadzin. The foundations of the fifth-century church thereby revealed show a plan similar to that of the still extant building erected in the seventh century, which takes the form of a square with four, salient axial niches, and four free-standing piers supporting the dome.

In the sixth and seventh centuries the wide use of the dome modified the basilican plan. In the aisleless churches the arches that support the drum of the dome rest on composite piers (Zovuni) or on short walls projecting from the north and south walls (Ptghni, T'alish). In the three-aisled basilicas the piers on which the arches rest are free-standing (Odzun, Bagavan, Mren, St Gayanē at Vagharshapat), constituting a cross within a square. The portions radiating from the central bay are vaulted

Fig. 13
Fig. 14

Plate 9

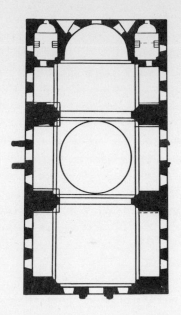
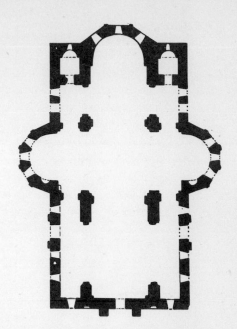

Figs. 13–16   *Top left: cathedral of T'alish, c. 668; bottom left: cathedral of Mren, 638–640; top right: cathedral of T'alin, seventh century; bottom right: church of Art'ik, seventh century (after Khatchatrian) 1 : 500*

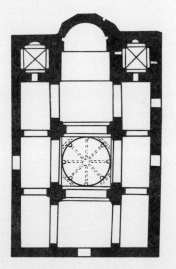
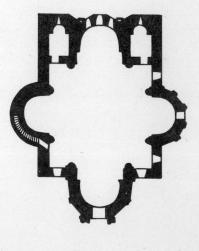

Fig. 15
Plate 10

higher than the aisles, consequently the cross shape is also expressed in the covering. At the cathedral of T'alin, recently restored, the north and south arms of the cross are extended to form corresponding niches or small apses, recalling a trefoil plan.

The strictly central plan appears in a number of variants. In its simplest form the square is buttressed by four salient niches, and the dome on squinches covers the entire central space (Agrak). When the niches are rectangular on the outside perimeter and there are no lateral chambers on the east end, the free-standing cross is more clearly expressed on the exterior.

Plate 11

Sometimes, as at Lmbat and the church of Ashtarak, known as Karmravor, the arms of the cross, except for the eastern one, also have a rectangular contour in the interior. The trefoil is a variant of the niche-buttressed square in which the west arm is longer and has a rectangular perimeter (Alaman, St Anania). In another variant of the same basic type, the diameters of the axial, saliant niches are smaller than the sides of the square,

Plate 12
Fig. 16

thus determining angular projections which provide eight points of support for the drum (Mastara, Art'ik, Voskepar). In all these churches the dome covers the entire central space but at the church of St John the Baptist at Bagaran, now almost completely destroyed, a different method had been used. The niches had a diameter that was again smaller than the sides of the square, but the dome which rested on four free-standing piers no longer covered the entire central space. This scheme had been used at Etchmiadzin, where, because of the larger dimensions of the building, the corner square spaces were equal to the central square.

Fig. 17

In its simplest form the niche-buttressed square is essentially a quatrefoil, and the finest example of a quatrefoil is the large church of Zvart'nots' erected between 644 and 652 by the Catholicos Nerses III, surnamed 'the Builder', next to his patriarchal palace. According to tradition, it was on this site, on the road to Vagharshapat, that King Trdat had met Gregory the Illuminator; hence the church was dedicated to the angels, the 'vigilant powers' (*zvart'nots'*) who had appeared to St Gregory in his vision. From the late fourth century on, quatrefoil structures had been erected, principally as *martyria*, in many parts of the world; they are to be found at Milan (San Lorenzo), in the Balkans (Peruštica), and in Syria at Seleucia Pieria, Apamea, Bosra and Aleppo to name only a few. In its over-all conception

Fig. 17   Plan of the church of Zvart'nots', 644–652 (after Khatchatrian)
1 : 500

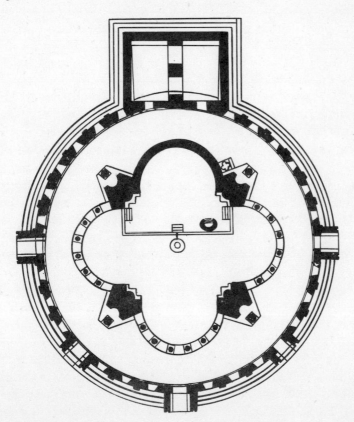

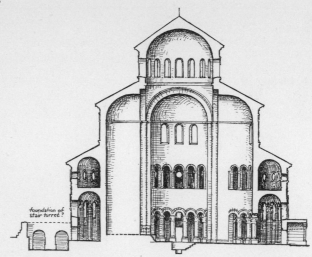

foundation of
stair turret?

Fig. 18   Sectional view of the church of Zvart'nots' (drawing by Kenneth J. Conant)

Fig. 17

Zvart'nots' ties in with these edifices, though differing from them in several respects. A circular ambulatory encompasses the lobes radiating from four massive piers, and a square chamber extends beyond this circular wall, on the east. Of the four lobes only the eastern one has a solid wall, the other three are open exedrae, each with six columns, and they give access to the ambulatory.

The church of Zvart'nots' was destroyed in the tenth century; now only the foundations, parts of the walls, the bases, capitals and sections of some of the columns remain, but comparison with other churches of similar design enabled Thoramanian to suggest a reconstruction which has been accepted by most *Fig. 18* scholars. The church rose to a great height, the walls above the exedrae were pierced by a series of arches which opened into the vaulted gallery of the ambulatory, and there were windows higher up in these exedrae walls. The dome with its circular drum, pierced by windows, rested by means of pendentives on

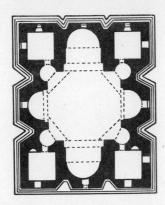

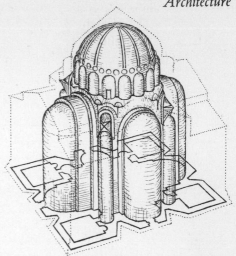

Figs. 19, 20   Vagharshapat; left, plan of the church of St Hrip'simē, 618 (after Khatchatrian)
1 : 500; right, envelope diagram of the same church (drawing by Kenneth J. Conant)

the arches connecting the four piers. It was abutted by the semi-domes of the quatrefoil, and these in turn were abutted by the vault of the gallery above the circular ambulatory.

The plan which more than any other has been considered as specifically Armenian is that of the church of St Hrip'sime at Vagharshapat. It represents an elaboration of the niche-buttressed square, in which four small cylindrical niches are lodged between the axial semicircular niches, giving access to four corner chambers. The dome covers the central octagonal space and it is abutted by both the axial and the diagonal niches. On the exterior, deep triangular niches mark the articulations of the design. The same type of structure is repeated with slight modifications in the church of St John at Sisian. The church of St Etchmiadzin at Soradir, known as the Red Church, shows what is probably an earlier stage of the development. There are no corner chambers on the west end, so that the axial and diagonal niches are clearly expressed on the exterior, while at

Fig. 19

Fig. 20

Plate 14

107

Fig. 11

the east end two narrow rectangular rooms flank the apse. At the church of Avan, on the contrary, the entire ensemble of chambers and niches is buried in the heavy masonry of a smooth-faced rectangular block, the corner chambers being circular instead of square as at St Hrip'simē. In these churches the addition of the diagonal niches determines an octagonal space, in others the octagon entirely replaces the central square and eight niches project from the eight sides (Irind, Zoravar).

This rapid survey shows the different solutions adopted by the Armenian architects of the sixth and seventh centuries in erecting a dome upon a square bay. Throughout this period Armenia was in contact with Persia, as well as with the eastern provinces of the Byzantine empire and with Georgia, where similar experimentation was taking place. The structural problems that the architects had to solve were the same, in particular in those areas where the building material was stone, as in Armenia. The mutual exchanges and counter-influences cannot all be clearly determined as yet, particularly since many of the connecting links with the past are missing. The temple of Garni lies outside the line of development of Armenian architecture, but there may also have existed centrally planned and domed mausolea which, as in other countries, could have served as prototypes. The point which should be stressed, however, is that in their experiments the Armenians frequently pursued an independent course.

When building activities were resumed in the Bagratid period, the architects had at their disposal the large repertory of structural forms created in the early centuries. Ani, the 'town of a thousand and one churches', protected by a double line of fortifications, was the most important centre; what is more King Gagik I had the good fortune to command the services of the architect Trdat. We do not know in what circumstances Trdat was asked to repair the dome of St Sophia of Constantinople, damaged by the earthquake of 989, but the fact that his assistance

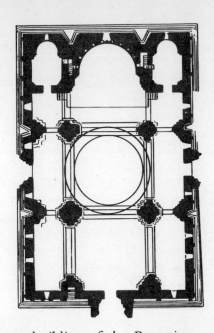

Fig. 21 Ani, cathedral, 989–1001 (after Khatchatrian) 1 : 500

was sought for the most famous building of the Byzantine empire is in itself a sufficient indication of his renown. At Ani, Trdat's master-work is the cathedral, erected between the years 989 and 1001. In this variant of the cross-in-a-rectangle plan, Trdat has stressed the vertical effect and the elegance of the general design. Pointed and stepped arches, rising from the free-standing, clustered piers, supported the circular drum on pendentives; the dome which rested on the drum is now destroyed. Recessed pilasters, placed against the north and south walls, face the central piers. The narrow lateral apses are almost entirely screened by short walls; ten semicircular arches open in the wall of the wide, central apse. The clustered piers of the cathedral of Ani recall those which were used later in Gothic architecture but they do not have the same structural function. On the exterior of the cathedral, the deep triangular recesses which mark the articulations of the design create areas of deep shadow and set off the elegance of the slender columns of the blind arcade. With its harmonious proportions, once dominated

Fig. 21

Plate 13

by the high dome, the cathedral of Ani deserves to be classed among the more important examples of medieval architecture.

In the church of St Gregory, also erected by Gagik I at Ani, Trdat had imitated the plan of the church of Zvart'nots'. Its foundations alone now remain and these show that Trdat had replaced the solid wall of the eastern niche of Zvart'nots' by an open exedra. Other churches of Ani offer examples of sex-foils and octofoils, usually with two lateral apses next to the eastern foil, and the entire construction is enclosed in a polygonal wall (ex. Church of the Redeemer) with, on occasion, triangular recesses between the foils (St Gregory of Abughamrents').

Fig. 22

Plate 15
Fig. 23

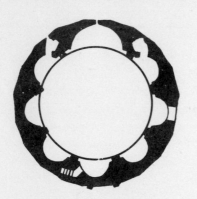

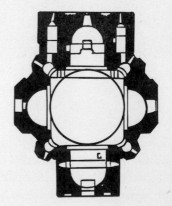

Figs. 22–24 Left, Ani, church of the Redeemer, 1035–1036; bottom left: Ani, church of St Gregory of Abughamrents'; bottom right: Aght'amar, church of the Holy Cross, 915–921 (after Khatchatrian) 1 : 350

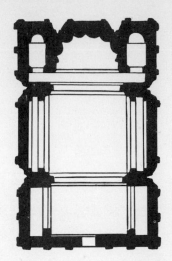

Fig. 25 Church of Marmashen,
c. 986–1029 (after Khatchatrian)
1 : 350

Adaptations of the niche-buttressed square, in which the niches are smaller than its sides, also appear during this period, for instance at the cathedral of Kars and at the church known as Kumbet Kilisse near that town. The plan of the church of the Holy Cross at Aght'amar, erected by King Gagik of Vas-purakan between the years 915 and 921, with semicircular axial niches, and cylindrical niches on the diagonals, if ultimately derived from the type represented by St Hrip'simē, is more akin to the church of Soradir in the province of Vaspurakan because in both cases there are no corner chambers, and narrow lateral apses flank the eastern apse. It was however the hall church, where the dome is supported by the piers projecting from the side walls, which, more than any other, became the favourite plan during this later period. The cathedral of Mar-mashen is one of the best preserved examples of this type.

The architects of the tenth and succeeding centuries did not always revert to the earlier models, sometimes developing more advanced types of construction. Large monastic complexes were erected during this period, for example at Tat'ev, in the province of Siunik', and at Sanahin and Haghbat in northern Armenia.

Plate 16

Fig. 24
Plate 17

Fig. 25
Plate 18

Fig. 26

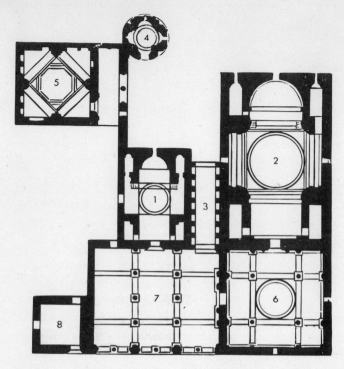

*Fig. 26   Monastery of Sanahin : 1, church of the Mother of God, tenth century ;
2, church of the Redeemer, 966 ; 3, vaulted hall known as the Academy of Gregory
Magistros ; 4, chapel of St Gregory, 1061 ; 5, library, 1063 ; 6, ante-chapel
(zhamatun), 1181 ; 7, ante-chapel, 1211 ; 8, bell tower, thirteenth century (after
Khatchatrian) 1 : 500*

These complexes comprised, besides the monks' cells, a library,
a refectory, a bell tower, several churches with large ante-
chapels *(zhamatuns)* and it is primarily in the latter that the new
methods of construction appear. The earliest known example
of this new type is, however, not an ante-chapel but the Shepherd's church built in the eleventh century, outside the walls of
Figs. 27, 28   Ani. The ground plan of this three-storied building takes the
form of a six-point star embedded in heavy masonry. On the

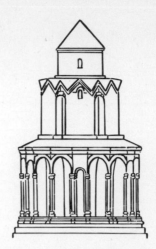

Figs. 27, 28 Ani, Shepherd's chapel, eleventh century. Envelope diagram and elevation (after Strzygowski) 1 : 200

exterior, twelve triangular recesses are cut in the walls, between the points of the star. Six arches, rising from the clustered piers at the angles of the star, meet at a central keystone and they bear the whole weight of the second storey. This storey is circular in the interior and hexagonal on the exterior, and above it rises the circular drum on which rests the conical dome.

Various systems of covering were used in the ante-chapels. In the one added to the south side of the church of the Holy Apostles at Ani, six columns abutting the walls divide the rectangular space into two square bays. Over each bay arches of masonry, resting on these columns, intersect one another diagonally, and short walls rising above the arches support the ceiling. The side walls are strengthened by wall-arches resting on low piers. A stalactite dome crowns the central space. More complex forms are used in the large square ante-chapel of the church of Horo-mos, built in 1038. The hall is spanned by two pairs of inter-secting arches running parallel with the side walls. Over the

Plate 19

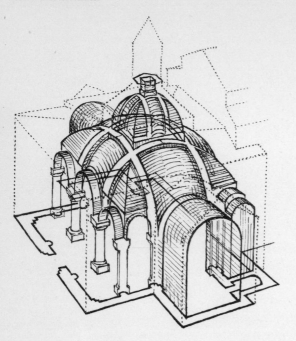

Fig. 29   Haghbat, ante-chapel (zhamatun), thirteenth century. Envelope diagram (drawing by Kenneth J. Conant)

bays to the east and west of the central square the ceiling rests on short walls rising above the arches as at the Holy Apostles of Ani, but the vaults of the lateral bays rest directly on the arches. The four corner rectangles are roofed with sections of triangular vaulting, intersecting each other at right angles. An octagonal drum, with a facing of carved slabs, rises above the central square and is crowned with a small dome carried on six small columns. As can be seen, different vaulting systems have been used here, and they reveal the initial stages of researches which culminated in the buildings of the twelfth and thirteenth cen-turies, such as the large ante-chapel of Haghbat. Large arches intersecting one another at right angles again span the square hall, but now the bays are roofed with vaults of masonry which rest directly on the arches.

Fig. 29

These cross-ribbed vaultings bear important testimony to the experiments carried out independently by the Armenian architects along lines similar to those undertaken in Western Europe. Some of the Armenian examples are of earlier date, but in both areas the builders were concerned with the same problem of providing adequate supports for the weight of heavy masonry vaults and they solved it in a comparable though not identical manner.

This method of construction favoured the creation of two- and three-storied buildings. The former are for the most part funerary chapels; the lower storey was used for burial, the upper one, usually of smaller size, was the chapel. Several of these churches were erected in the course of the eleventh-fourteenth centuries, principally in the province of Siunik'. One of the most richly decorated is the chapel of Noravank' at Amaghu. The three-storied buildings are bell-towers erected in the large monastic complexes. At the monastery of Haghbat the lower stories have one or more small chapels for the religious services, and the belfry above was crowned with a conical roof. In all these buildings the vertical effect has been stressed, and the architects tend to give less massive proportions to the monuments.

Plate 20

Plate 21

With the development of the transit trade during the Bagratid and later periods caravanserais and hostelries were built on the main routes in different parts of the country. The caravanserais are principally three-aisled, vaulted basilicas, covered by a single roof. There are no windows in the walls, and light and air enter only through the small openings in the roof. The ruins of a caravanserai near T'alin reveal a more complex structure. The large central area was open and it was surrounded by a vaulted gallery on three sides and five small rooms on the north side, all of which opened directly onto the central square. Three-aisled basilican halls flanked this central area, but they were not connected. The large hostelry of Ani consisted of two separate but adjoining buildings. In each the central, rectangular hall was lined on either side by small rooms, opening directly onto the hall. The large rooms on the short ends of the rectangle are believed to have served as shops. In the north-western corner of the town of Ani are the ruins of a palace, probably erected in the thirteenth century; though the scale is smaller, we have here a further example of a building with rooms surrounding a central hall. The large portal still retains part of the elaborate decoration of red and black stone inlays, and delicately carved star motifs and interlaces.

Armenian architecture constitutes one of the vital and important chapters in the story of Christian architecture. Throughout the centuries we see the architects seeking to solve in a variety of ways the structural problems of domed stone buildings, and several of the centrally-planned churches have a distinctly original character. In contact with East and West, Armenia benefited from the experiments carried on in other countries, but she always translated such elements as she adopted into her own national idiom. In the opinion even of those scholars who rightfully reject the extreme claims made by Strzygowski, Armenian architectural forms at times penetrated into other countries and influenced their designs; one example of this is the tenth-century Byzantine church type, where the dome above the square bay is carried by corner squinches. As R. Krautheimer has expressed it in his recent work on Early Christian and Byzantine Architecture: 'Of all the border countries of the Empire, Armenia is the only one to deal with Byzantine architecture on an equal footing. But the differences between Byzantine and Armenian buildings—in design, construction, scale and decoration—cannot be too strongly stressed.'

CHAPTER VIII

Sculpture

THE wholesale destruction of the temples and idols after the establishment of Christianity has deprived us of almost all vestiges of pagan statuary. The bronze head of Aphrodite found at Erzinjan is the only surviving example of the statues which, according to tradition, were brought from the Hellenistic cities by Tigran the Great. Some Greek works may have been known in Armenia during the Orontid period when the country was under Seleucid suzerainty but we have no evidence of this. The first impact of Hellenistic art appears on the coins struck by Tigran the Great and by his immediate successors. The obverse of these coins bears the portrait of the ruler, in profile, and almost always beardless. He wears the head-dress known as the Armenian tiara. This consists of a bonnet in the form of a truncated cone around which is wound the royal diadem decorated with addorsed birds at the sides of a star; the lappets of the bonnet fall over the shoulders. On the finer examples the head is carefully modelled, on others the forms are slightly flattened. Stamped on the reverse are the customary Greek types such as the Tyche of Antioch after the famous statue by Eutychides, a pupil of Lysippus; Zeus *nikephoros*; a standing Nike; Heracles leaning on his club; or Nike in a quadriga. Recent studies have divided some of the coins of Tigran the Great into three principal groups: I, coins with the legend *basileos Tigranou,* and the Tyche of Antioch, minted in Antioch; II, coins with the legend *Basileos basileou Tigranou,* with the same Tyche, minted in Armenia; III, coins with the legend *basileos Tigranou,* and a different Tyche, minted at Damascus. According to the observations of H. Seyrig the second group must have been minted at Artaxata, which was built on a river, so that the Tyche represents that of Artaxata and the

Plate 5

Plate 24

river at her feet is the Arax. A Greek type was thus adapted to a specific Armenian locality. Two bronze coins of Tigran the Great, found at Nisibis, bear a large tree on the reverse. Seyrig suggests that this unusual type may represent an oracular tree, and one is reminded of an old custom in Armenia whereby the future was foretold by the movements of the leaves of the *Sosi* tree planted in the sacred grove of Armavir. On the reverse of a small bronze coin, which may also be attributed to Tigran the Great, a horse has been stamped, a type which is distinctly Parthian and not Greek.

Though slight in themselves, these divergencies suggest three ways in which the Armenians modified the Greek models: by giving a different meaning to the types they adopted, by sub stituting for them iconographic themes which belonged to Armenian mythology, or by replacing them with types borrowed from the Parthians.

The general artistic trend of the Artaxiad period in Armenia must have been similar, in many respects, to the one in Comma gene known to us through the *hierothesion* or temple tomb of Antiochus I at Nimrud Dagh. The reliefs on which Antiochus, wearing the Armenian tiara, stands before a deity, clasping him by the hand, show the blending of the Achaemenian and Greek artistic traditions. The compositions are typical of Iranian scenes of investiture, the costumes are also Iranian, while stylistically the classical forms have been modified to conform to Iranian aesthetic conventions.

Several gold medallions, depicting a female bust, found at Armavir, in Armenia, reveal a similar modification of forms. However Armenia, long under Iranian suzerainty, must have felt the influence of Iranian art even more than Commagene. No Achaemenian monuments have come to light in Armenia, but a few Iranian rock reliefs are known through sketches made by travellers in the nineteenth century. At Bayazid two men (magi?) stand on either side of an altar which bears an animal.

Fig. 30

On a rock near Lake Urmia two Sasanian kings, probably
Ardashir I and Shapur I, are represented on horseback, and
before each stands a man, perhaps an Armenian king. At
Boshat a king on horseback is followed by a bearded man, on
foot.

These few examples suggest the general background against
which one must view the development of Armenian sculpture.
Classical influence was still strong in the first century AD.
At the temple of Garni, the rich acanthus scrolls, with interposed lion masks and occasional palmettes, the fine Ionic and
acanthus capitals, the other floral and geometric ornaments, are
typical of the contemporary monuments of Asia Minor.

Plates 22, 23

Fig. 30   Rock relief from Bayazid

Fig. 31

Fig. 32

Fig. 31 Relief from the Hypogaeum of Aghts', 364 (after Arak'elian)

A few iconographic themes of antiquity still survived in the Christian period. On one of the slabs of the hypogaeum of the Arsacid kings built at Aghts' in AD 364 a nude man thrusts his lance into a wild boar which is also attacked by two dogs. This scene is derived from the Hellenistic funerary repertory and examples of the hero hunting an animal are to be found in the chapels of Kerch in the Crimea and Marissa in Palestine, on the sarcophagi from Sidon and on later monuments. But in the clumsy carving of Aghts' all feeling for the classical form is lost, the figure in very low relief stands in a frontal position and only his feet are shown in profile. The heads in tufa, discovered in and around Dvin, and which originally belonged to large statues, show the same disregard for the subtleties of modelling. The head-dress, in the shape of a truncated cone, with an all-over diaper or chevron design, recalls the Armenian tiara, but it has no diadem or lappets. Though totally devoid of artistic quality these heads are important vestiges of early statuary and may have been intended to portray the kings of Armenia.

In the sculpture of the fifth–seventh centuries the Oriental trend prevailed. Although frontality of the figures is less rigidly observed than in Parthian art, the compositions are rarely unified, they consist rather in the juxtaposition of separate elements. Decorative interest is the prime consideration, as is shown by the way in which the figures are sometimes distorted in order to fill all available space, as well as by the treatment of the draperies. The parallel grooves cut at different angles create linear patterns, while the sharp oppositions of light and shade produce a colouristic effect. The artist's lack of interest in conveying the solidity of the human form contrasts with the care taken over getting the details of the costume right whenever contemporary figures are portrayed.

Fig. 32   Stone heads found at Dvin, probably from royal effigies. Height 38 and 28 cm. respectively (after Arak'elian)

The carved steles known as cross-stones *(khatchk'ar)* constitute the most original group of this early period. More than seventy of these funerary or votive stones, many in fragmentary condition, have been discovered in different parts of Armenia, often close to basilican churches. They take the form of rectangular pillars mounted on cubic bases; a slight hollow in the top of the pillars leads one to suppose that originally an iron or stone cross was inserted there.

Plates 25–27   Carved on the four faces of the pillars and of the bases are individual figures of Christ, saints and angels; the Virgin alone with the Christ child or between two angels; scenes from the Old and New Testaments; large crosses sometimes framed by leaves; and a variety of floral and geometric ornaments. The Biblical scenes—Daniel in the den of lions, the sacrifice of Isaac, the three Jewish Youths in the fiery furnace—belong to the repertory of Early Christian funerary art. No guiding principle can be discerned in the choice of the rare Gospel scenes. More interesting are the representations of a purely national character,

Plate 28   inspired by the story of the conversion of King Trdat. Time and again the king is portrayed with a pig's head, that is, in the aspect he is supposed to have assumed before his conversion.

In certain of the compositions the lions at the sides of Daniel sometimes stand on their front legs and their body slants upwards, or else they are seated erect on their hind legs, thus recalling the old Oriental Gilgamesh motif. The Oriental influence is also evident in a male figure holding with upraised hands a rectangle decorated with roundels whose pose recalls that of Anahit on a Sasanian capital from Tag-i-Bostan; like-

Fig. 33   wise in a nimbed man holding a book, who is attired in the typical Iranian costume.

In a second group of cross-stones the shafts attain a height of three or four metres and the scenes, carved one above the other, are enclosed in rectangular frames. The general design is curiously similar to that of Northumbrian panelled crosses, and the

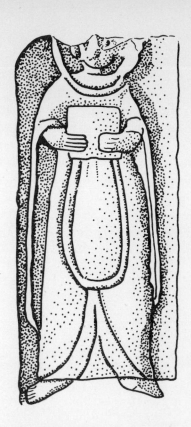

*Fig. 33   Stele from T'alin
(after Hovsep'ian)*

attention of scholars has been arrested by this similarity between two groups of monuments so far removed from and independent of one another. At Odzun, the two shafts, erected between the arches raised on a high podium, form part of a funerary monument. Floral and geometric ornaments cover the lateral faces, while saints and other figures, including that of King Trdat in his porcine aspect, are carved on the front and back of the shafts.

The stone architecture of Armenia, like that of neighbouring Georgia, provided an opportunity to adorn the façades with relief sculpture. The application of both figurative and ornamental compositions distinguish the Caucasian churches from other monuments of the East Christian world. In the rare

Fig. 34 Church of Ptghni. Portrait of the founder Amatuni, sixth century (after Arak'elian)

instances in which such adornments appear on Byzantine churches, they consist of carved marble slabs inserted in the brick architecture. In Asia Minor, though the architecture was of stone, sculpture was rarely used. The delicate carvings on the Syrian churches are primarily ornamental, and in Coptic Egypt the figure sculpture used at an early date soon disappeared.

The figural reliefs of the façades often recall the themes which, in the Early Christian period, were used in painting or in mosaics inside the churches. Thus the carving on the tympanum of the west portal of Mren, which shows Christ standing between saints being approached by the donors, is a typical apse composition. The flying angels carrying the *imago clypeata* of Christ, and the busts of saints in medallions carved around a window of the church of Ptghni repeat the decoration of an apse arch. The quarter-length figure of Christ, or the Virgin and Child, represented in other churches, are also related to apse paintings.

The *nakharars* who erected the churches wished to have their memory perpetuated through their images. Various iconographic formulas have been adopted for these donor portraits. At Mren, the founder, David Saharuni, and another man, probably the

feudal lord of the province, Nerseh Kamsarakan, turn, hands
extended in prayer, towards the central group of Christ and
saints. At Mahmudchugh, near Harich, the donor stands next
to the large figure of the Virgin and Child adored by angels.
At Ptghni, Manuel Amatuni, on horseback, shoots an arrow
at a lion, while a younger man pierces a lion with his lance.
The hero of Aghts', represented in the nude killing a boar,
was derived from Hellenistic art, whereas the lion hunt of Ptghni
is related to one of the favourite themes of Sasanian royal iconography. Exceptionally, at Zvart'nots' the secular figures set
in the spandrels of the arches do not represent the founder of the
church. These men, who hold hammers, spades and other
instruments are, in all probability, the workmen who took part
in the construction, while the cleric Yohan (John), whose
name is inscribed next to him, must be the architect.

Plate 30

Fig. 34

Fig. 35

Fig. 36

Figs. 35, 36   Church of Zvart'nots', seventh century. Left, figure of a workman in one of the spandrels; right, carving of the architect Yohan (after Arak'elian)

Plate 29

Figural representations occasionally appear on the capitals and on the lintels. On a lintel from Dvin the classical composition of putti gathering grapes has been transformed into an actual vintage scene, but the interest in reality is only apparent in the subject itself and not in its rendering. In a desire to fill the entire background the sculptor has enlarged, out of proportion, the leaves of the vine and the clusters of grapes. This *horror vacui* is one of the characteristic traits of Armenian art and indeed, generally speaking, of all Near Eastern sculpture. Different artistic trends were at work in this formative period.

Plate 31

Plate 32

The majestic eagles on the capitals of Zvart'nots' are among the finest examples of seventh-century Armenian sculpture, and the rendering in high relief of the Ionic volutes which surmount the basket capitals is good; at Dvin during the same period, the volutes of similar capitals have become interlacing circles carved in low relief.

Plate 34

The repertory of ornamental motifs is fairly restricted during this period. The palmette scroll and a stylized vine scroll, with a large leaf and a bunch of grapes interposed between the circumvolutions, are among the favourite elements from plant life. Pomegranate branches laden with large fruits sometimes spread in the spandrels of the arches, or cover the arch itself. The linear interlaces are not yet much developed. The small horseshoe arches, sometimes with a bird lodged under each arch, are among the most characteristic designs. The relative simplicity of the ornaments accords well with the style of the monuments; sculpture is throughout subordinated to the architecture and serves to stress the constituent elements. The linear treatment of the carvings is also consistent with this aim and respects the uniform surfaces of the walls.

Plate 17

The church of the Holy Cross erected by King Gagik Artsruni on the island of Aght'amar in Lake Van, between AD 914 and 921, marks the resumption of artistic activity in this area. This outstanding monument is a unique example in the Christian

art of this period of a church with all-over decoration on the
exterior. A frieze of running animals is carved under the pyramidal roof of the dome and a second one under the eaves of the
church. An elaborate vine scroll, inhabited by animals and
enlivened by scenes of hunting and of rural life, skirts the walls
above the windows, having as its central group a king, seated
cross-legged, drinking and plucking grapes, and attended by
two servants.

Plate 34

Larger figures occupy the taller wall surfaces. On the west
façade King Gagik proffers to Christ the model of the church
he had built, a seraph stands at each side, and large crosses, one
of them held by two angels, recall that the edifice was dedicated
to the Holy Cross. The apostles who preached the Gospel in
Armenia, and Gregory the Illuminator, are grouped with other
saints on the east façade. Old Testament scenes, images of
Christ, the Virgin, prophets and saints, cover the north and
south walls. Under the central gable of each façade appears the
large figure of an evangelist. Real and imaginary animals
alternate with these representations and some are carved in the
round above them; ornate bands frame the windows and the
triangular niches, and a wider band runs below the pictorial
reliefs. Figures and ornaments are carved in fairly high relief,
although there is little surface modelling. The overlapping folds
of the draperies are flattened, but in general the lines follow the
shapes of the limbs, and the linear patterns tend to reveal the
form of the body instead of covering it with an over-all design.
The sculptors of Aght'amar show a better understanding of the
elements of the classical drapery than did those of the preceding
period and the stylization is never carried to extremes. Despite
a certain awkwardness, these figures presented in frontal or
three-quarter view, impress the spectator by the dignity of their
posture and by the intense gaze of their large almond-shaped
eyes. The spiritual content of this art far outweighs its formal
merits.

Plate 36

Plate 35

The sudden appearance of this rich ensemble must have been due to the personal initiative of King Gagik who wished to have a church equalling in its sumptuousness the rich decorations of the palace he had built on the same island of Aght'amar. The earlier monuments of Armenia provided a limited range of figural compositions and the artists had to draw their inspiration from a variety of sources. The feasting scene at the centre of the vine scroll is ultimately derived from one of the favourite themes of Sasanian royal iconography, perpetuated also in Muslim art. The presence of this group and of the secular scenes of the vine scroll on the façade of a church is to be explained by the fact that this was a palatine chapel, and similar representations adorned the throne chamber of the palace. The survival of Sasanian motifs is apparent in the types and rendering of the animals, in particular the whale in the Jonah cycle which has been transformed into the Persian senmurv or hippocamp. The influence of contemporary Muslim art can be discerned in some of the other animals, and that of Byzantine iconography in the religious scenes. These elements have however been fused together in an ensemble which in its final result differs from these various artistic trends and stands out as an original conception. As in earlier Armenian monuments, the details of the contemporary costumes are carefully depicted. King Gagik's crown, a variant of the Sasanian winged type, is no doubt the one he had received from the Caliph; his long tunic is decorated with rows of concentric and interlocking circles while the pattern of his heavy mantle consists of circles framing birds, with leaves placed in the lozengeshaped spaces between these circles. The portraits of the two Artsruni princes who were martyred for their faith by the Arabs appear on the south façade; they are clad in long mantles fashioned from costly and ornate material. The same type of Oriental costume, used at the time in Armenia, has been extended to Saul in the scene of the fight between David and Goliath, where he wears a large turban.

Plate 34

Plate 35

Plate 36

The church of Aght'amar remains an isolated example. Unheralded by earlier monuments, it also lacked imitators in the centuries that followed. A few Gospel scenes, figures of Christ, saints and angels decorated the eleventh-century church of Noravank' of Bghen in the province of Siunik'. Neither in the extent of the decoration nor in the quality of the sculptures can this church compare with Aght'amar. The figures are short and heavy with large faces devoid of expression, and the compositions consist of juxtaposed units.

The sculptors of the thirteenth and fourteenth centuries reverted to the earlier practice of placing the figural representa- tions in the tympanum over the portal. Christ between saints, the Virgin and Child, sometimes framed by two angels, are the favourite themes. Occasionally a scene from the Bible has been represented, for instance at Hohanna Vank' where the Wise and Foolish Virgins stand at either side of the enthroned Christ. In a few instances portraits of the apostles are carved at the sides of the portal, or in the arch above it. Figural sculpture was also used inside the buildings. At the church of the White Virgin the Byzantine iconographic theme of the Deesis is developed on five separate slabs: Christ enthroned is on the central slab, and at His sides the Virgin, John the Baptist and two apostles stand in three-quarter view in the attitude of prayer or supplication.

As in the preceding period, the donor portraits constitute the most interesting group. The portrait of King Gagik I of Ani, now lost, and which once decorated the church of St Gregory he had built, is the only known Armenian free-standing statue to have been carved entirely in the round. Judging from old photographs this must have been a work of real artistic merit and one senses that the face, with its noble expression, was a faithful portrait of this ruler. In three other churches at Haghbat, Sanahin and Harich respectively, the portraits of the two donors, holding a model of the church or an icon of the Virgin, are placed in a niche of the east façade. Although carved in the

Plate 37

Plate 38

round, these niche-statues produce the impression of a flat relief for there is no surface modelling on their vestments. In the tympanum of the forechurch of Aisasi (AD 1270), the donors stand in the attitude of prayer on either side of the Virgin and Child. Stylization of the forms and the linear treatment of the draperies are here carried to extremes. In the small church of the Virgin at Noravank' built in 1339, the donors, one of whom carries the model of the church, also flank the Virgin and Child, but here the figures carved in high relief are attached to columns. These are unique examples in Armenian sculpture, recalling the column statues on the façades of Romanesque churches.

In the thirteenth and fourteenth centuries the early icono-graphic types of the Sasanian royal hunt, perpetuated in Muslim art, were occasionally used by the Armenian artists for the donor portraits carved in the tympana. The rider sometimes impales a wild animal with his lance, or else he severs the head of a lion, or again, armed with a bow, he turns round in his saddle to shoot an arrow. The dedicatory idea is absent from these representations in which one does not see the model of the church or Christ or the Virgin in whose honour the edifice has

Fig. 37

been erected. The interest in decoration prevalent in this period also brings about modifications in some of the compositions. At the church of Tanahat, a peacock, a small bird and a quadruped fill the space above the rider and the lion; the secular element is thus emphasized to the detriment of the religious significance of the scene.

The delicate balance between carved ornaments and architecture still persisted in the tenth and eleventh centuries, although the bands of interlace which frame the windows and doors are considerably wider. But increasingly, in the following centuries, the decoration tends to cover the façades and to lose its close connection with the architectural members. Ornament becomes an end in itself, and is not subordinated to architecture.

The simpler forms of linear interlaces, used in the fifth–seventh centuries, were fully developed in the Bagratid period. Interweaving and interlocking strands determine a number of geometric figures such as triangles, lozenges, circles and rectangles, without interrupting the continuity of the design. This type of polygonal interlace was also used in the ensuing centuries, but together with such examples one finds others, where the interlace is fragmented and consequently the polygonal units are isolated and juxtaposed. Bands of star motifs, a favourite type of ornament of Seljuk art, are increasingly used, each star being filled with palmettes or with real and imaginary birds. Among the latter, sirens and human-headed griffins occur most frequently. Ornamental stalactites also make their appearance during the thirteenth and fourteenth centuries; they cover the interiors of the domes, especially in the rock-cut churches of Geghard, and sometimes the squinches and arches as well.

New types or new developments are also to be observed in the floral ornaments. In the few instances where the acanthus is still used, the leaves, usually placed erect side by side, are flattened and covered by parallel grooves. The vine scroll rarely appears; instead, rigid vine stocks, with interlocking bunches of grapes, are aligned so as to cover a fairly large area, such as a tympanum. The palmette has now become the favourite motif, either in the simpler form of a narrow interlacing scroll, or in more complex circumvolutions over a wide space. These palmette scrolls also occasionally fill the entire background of the tympana on which the Virgin and Child or other compositions have been represented.

Animals depicted alone, or confronted, or fighting one another, appear more frequently in the sculpture of this later period. They sometimes run through the foliage, as in the spandrels of the blind arcade around the church of St Gregory built by Tigran Honents' of Ani in 1215. At other times they are set under the arches which circle the drum of the dome, or they are carved above the doors.

All these geometric, floral and animal motifs are abundantly used in the interiors of the churches as well, and they are sometimes combined with figural representations. For instance at the monastery of Horomos, near Ani, built in AD 1038, eight richly carved slabs line the octagonal drum of the dome of the forechurch. An abbreviated composition of the Last Judgment occupies the central eastern slab: Christ enthroned is surrounded by the four symbols of the Evangelists and two rows of nimbed figures stand below Him. Two ornate crosses flank the central slab, the others are decorated with interlaces, a fret design and stylized vine stocks. Various ornaments are carved on the arches of the forechurch, and on those of other churches, as well as on different architectural members such as engaged columns or squinches.

The greatest variety of ornamental designs is to be found on the cross-stones *(khatchk'ar)* which from the ninth century on Plate 39 are flat rectangular slabs carved only on one face. A large cross—plain, striated or plaited—occupies the central field. It usually rests on an ornate medallion and it is framed by two leaves whose surfaces are covered with linear or floral interlaces.

The rectangular bands around the slab are decorated with a linear interlace; these bands may however be replaced by a succession of star motifs, or square and rectangular compartments filled with floral or geometric motifs. Christ is sometimes represented in the upper band, together with saints. Both the cross and the ornaments stand out against the dark shadow of the background which has been cut away and the best examples produce the effect of a delicate lace-work.

The imaginative powers of the Armenian sculptors in the field of ornamentation and their technical skill in transferring to the stone these constantly renewed designs find their finest expression in these cross-stones. On the larger slabs the Crucifixion takes the place of the cross and palmette interlaces fill all the available space between the figures of Christ, the Virgin and Saint John. This same type of ornate background was used in Islamic art, in metalwork or in ivory and wood carvings.

Plate 41

Geometric designs, principally polygonal interlaces, and real and fabulous animals were also executed in stucco for the decoration of the palaces and the houses of the rich merchants. Several fragments were discovered at Ani and an even larger number at Dvin, dating for the most part in the twelfth and thirteenth centuries. The griffins, lions and dogs running in a floral scroll, or the sirens and human-headed winged quadrupeds recall those represented in contemporary Seljuk art, but similar designs had been used at an earlier date in Armenian manuscripts and occasionally in wood-carvings. Animals pursuing one another in the midst of a floral scroll decorate the lateral bands which frame the doors of the monastery of the Holy Apostles at Mush, executed in 1134. Rider saints, one of whom probably represents Saint George killing the dragon, adorn the upper band of the frame. On the door itself the decoration consists of polygonal interlaces determined by the extension of the sides of a six-point star. A few other carved doors have survived. On some of these the general design, with a central cross, framed

Plate 42

by floral and geometric motifs, repeats the type of composition of the stone steles.

The greater part of the precious vessels donated to the churches and monasteries has been destroyed and only a few reliquaries and silver bindings have survived. Thanks to these we can also obtain some idea of the minor arts of the Kingdom of Cilicia, where no stone sculpture of any significance has come to light. Plates 43, 44 On a large reliquary in the shape of a triptych, made at the monastery of Skevra in 1293, Christ on the cross, executed in high relief, occupies the central panel, while the Annunciation, figures of saints standing or enclosed in medallions, are embossed on both sides of the two wings. The delicate style of these figures, the interest in naturalism, are traits that characterize the miniature painting in Cilician manuscripts. Two silver bindings, dated respectively to 1254 and 1255, show the skill of the silversmiths working at the patriarchal see of Hromkla. The upper cover of the binding of 1254 is decorated with the figure of Christ on the cross, framed by four standing evangelists Plate 45 and the busts of eight apostles in medallions, while on the lower cover Christ is enthroned in an ornate quatrefoil and the symbols of the evangelists, in the midst of floral scrolls, occupy the four corners. The compositions are well ordered, especially if one eliminates the crosses and other small plaques which were added later. On the binding of 1255 (Erevan, *Matenadaran*, no. 7690) the figures are much larger and occupy almost the entire surface of each plate. The Byzantine iconographic theme of the *Deesis*, that is Christ standing between the Virgin and John the Baptist, is represented on the upper cover, and the four evangelists in frontal or three-quarter view are aligned on the lower cover. The compositions of the Crucifixion and the Nativity which adorn the gilt silver binding made at Sis in 1334 (Jerusalem, Armenian Patriarchate, no. 2649) are embossed in higher relief. Because of the crowding of the figures which cover the entire surface, the general effect is less pleasing, although the individual elements are executed with great skill.

A few silver bindings and reliquaries made in Great Armenia have also survived. The most interesting is the triptych commissioned in 1300 by the feudal lord Eatchi Proshian, and decorated with the embossed figures of Christ, angels, saints and the bust of the donor in the attitude of the orans. The delicacy of style, peculiar to the art of the silversmiths, differentiates these figures from the contemporary stone sculpture and relates them more closely to the Cilician examples. We must finally mention a few bronze censers found at Ani, decorated with the principal episodes of the life of Christ. Although their execution is somewhat coarse, these censers are interesting as the only extant examples, other than painting, on which a fairly extensive Gospel cycle may be seen.

Plate 47

CHAPTER IX

Painting

THE EXCAVATIONS at the Baths built at Garni in the third century AD have brought to light the pavement mosaic of one of the rooms, the only extant example of the pictorial art of the pagan period in Armenia. The mosaic measures 2.90 by 2.90 metres. Personifications of the Ocean and the Sea, portrayed as busts and now badly damaged, occupy the central panel, and all around are represented, on a green ground recalling the sea, different deities and allegorical figures identified by Greek inscriptions. The major part of the mosaic is destroyed. There remain however several Nereids riding on Tritons, sea gods such as Glaukos, the allegory of the Abyss (Bathos), a winged nude figure holding a fish net, all depicted in the somewhat debased style of late Antiquity.

Fig. 38

Fragmentary remains excavated at Dvin and elsewhere show that the Armenians continued to employ this mode of decoration in the succeeding centuries. The best preserved examples are however to be found outside Armenia, in the Armenian churches and monasteries established in Jerusalem during the Early Christian period. The largest of these pavement mosaics with Armenian inscriptions lay in a church near the Damascus Gate. It represents a luxuriant vine scroll issuing from an amphora and inhabited by a variety of birds. Mosaics were also used for wall decorations. Fragments of a portrayal of the Virgin and Child were discovered in the apse of the seventh-century cathedral at Dvin, and remnants of a similar representation were brought to light at Zvart'nots'. The latter were not found *in situ*, but we have the evidence of the tenth-century Arab writer al Mukkadasi that the image of the Virgin was visible on entering the church. It must therefore have adorned the apse as at Dvin and in Byzantine churches.

Fig. 38 Garni, the Bath. Detail of pavement mosaic, third century (after Izmailova and Aivazian)

The use of mosaics must have been confined to very important churches; the more usual medium was painting. In a treatise directed against an Armenian iconoclastic sect, written at the end of the sixth century or in the early seventh, the author, Vrt'anes K'ert'ogh, upholds the dictum that 'all that the Holy Scriptures relate is painted in the churches'. He specifically mentions the Nativity, Baptism, the Passion, Crucifixion, Entombment, Resurrection and Ascension, the image of the Virgin and Child, scenes from the lives of saints, in particular the stoning of St Stephen, episodes from the martyrdom of St Gregory the Illuminator and that of the saints Hrip'simē and Gayanē. No such detailed cycle has been preserved in monu, ments of the corresponding period. In several churches a com, position inspired by the visions of Ezekiel and Isaiah fills the apse. At Lmbat, Christ enthroned in an aureole is flanked by double wheels surrounded by flames, by a tetramorph and by a six,winged seraph. Remnants of a composition at T'alin, which probably represented the Entry into Jerusalem, provide the only corroborative evidence of Vrt'anes K'ert'ogh's state, ment concerning the existence of a Gospel cycle. Standing figures of saints appear on the lower part of the apse wall at

Plate 46

T'alish, T'alin and Mren, and in these last two churches medallion portraits of saints surround the apse arch.

The general evolution of Armenian painting can be traced primarily through illuminated manuscripts. These are fortunately very numerous, in fact surprisingly so when one considers the hazards of constant warfare and the religious persecutions. In their accounts the historians sometimes recall the destruction of large collections, and one such mention will convey an idea of the extent of the losses. According to Stephen Orbelian, when the Seljuks captured the fortress of Baghaberd in 1170 they destroyed more than ten thousand manuscripts brought there for safekeeping from the churches and monasteries of Siunik'. The vast production of manuscripts can be partly explained by the supreme importance Armenians attached to them. A copy of the Scriptures or of a liturgical book was regarded by its owner as an imperishable treasure set up in heaven. By offering it to a church or to a monastery the donor increased his hopes of salvation, since his name featured from that time on in the daily prayers. The act of copying or of commissioning a manuscript is sometimes compared to that of erecting a church or fashioning a cross, and praised as a pious deed. Miraculous powers were attributed to some Gospel manuscripts, particularly during the later centuries, and they came to be known by special names, such as 'the Saviour of all', or the 'Ressurector of the dead'. A manuscript which fell into the hands of the infidels was said to be captive and it was the duty of a faithful Christian to redeem it, just as he would ransom a prisoner. Time and again the scribes, in the notices they added to the manuscripts, enjoin the owner to bury them in time of war. Pious men and women from all stations of life desired to have, as their most prized possession, a Gospel manuscript or a psalter, an illuminated one if possible, and the notices have sometimes preserved touching accounts of entire families, and even of some of their friends, joining forces in order to acquire this great treasure.

These notices also record the difficulties encountered by the monks in the pursuit of their work when, fleeing the invasions, they carried with them a manuscript which they had begun to copy in one monastery, had continued in another, and completed sometimes in yet a third.

It seems very probable that in the period of intense activity which followed the invention of the alphabet, painters occasionally collaborated with the scribes, using as models illustrated Greek manuscripts which had been brought to Armenia. In his anti-iconoclastic treatise, Vrt'anes K'ert'ogh speaks of Gospel manuscripts in purple vellum, painted in gold and silver and bound with ivory plaques; one such sumptuous copy must have come from the imperial city, and the Early Christian ivory book covers preserved as the binding of the tenth-century Gospel of Etchmiadzin corroborates the evidence furnished by Vrt'anes. Moreover, the ornamental frames of the canon tables of the Etchmiadzin Gospel, which appear to have retained more faithfully than contemporary Greek or Latin manuscripts the original decorative scheme devised for the Eusebian canon tables, also suggest the presence in Armenia of illuminated Greek manuscripts of an early date.

Plate 48

It was natural for Christian Armenia to seek models for her religious art in the important cities of the Byzantine empire, and the Western trend which had started at the time of Tigran the Great and continued in the subsequent centuries was kept alive by the influence of Early Christian models. However, the remains of the wall paintings, and even more clearly two leaves from an illustrated Gospel of the late sixth or the early seventh century, the only extant examples of the illumination of this period, clearly show by their style that the survival of the Parthian tradition and the influence of Sasanian art must also be taken into account. The Adoration of the Magi, one of the four Gospel scenes that are preserved, best shows the merging of these two trends in Armenian art: the iconography, with the

Plate 50   Virgin seated between the Magi introduced by an angel, and the architectural setting of the niche flanked by colonnades are derived from Early Christian models, but the Magi themselves, in their facial type, costume and especially their characteristic stance, with the knees bent outward and heels joined, are direct descendants of Sasanian models.

The subtle blending of these two artistic strains characterizes the Armenian style. In general the Armenian artists tend to simplify and to stylize the human figure; their primary concern is rarely the imitation of nature, they prefer to stress the decora-tive character of the individual figures as well as of the entire composition, and there can be no denying the fact that their works frequently gain in expressive intensity through this process of simplification.

A work of outstanding quality marks the resumption of artistic activity after the centuries of Arab occupation; this is

Plate 53   the Gospel known as that of Queen Mlk'ē, as the consort of King Gagik of Vaspurakan was called, a manuscript illustrated in 862, probably for a member of the Artsruni family, and offered later by the Queen to the monastery of Varag. The

Plate 52   Nilotic scenes of a crocodile hunt, the octopuses and other sea fish that fill the lunettes of the canon tables, the architectonic character of the arcades supported by sturdy columns imitating marble or porphyry, all point to the use of a model of the Early Christian period, perhaps of Alexandrian origin. The portraits of the Evangelists, and the Ascension, which no doubt was one of several Gospel scenes originally placed at the beginning of the manuscript, are painted in imitation of the impressionistic style of late classical art, the modelling of the forms being achieved through colour contrasts rather than through gradual shading. However, in the majestic and severe figure of Christ seated in an aureole between two archangels attired in the Byzantine imperial costume, the Armenian tendency towards stylization comes to the fore.

This tendency is even more marked in the paintings executed half a century later at the church on the island of Aght'amar erected by Gagik of Vaspurakan, the only Armenian church which has retained, almost in its entirety, its painted decoration. An extensive Gospel cycle, beginning with the Annunciation and continuing to the Last Judgment, runs around the walls on two zones; portraits of bishops cover the surfaces of the piers and of the diagonal niches. The painting of the apse has disappeared and only the apostles portrayed on the semicircular wall remain. The original dome was destroyed, but on the drum one can still see a few scenes relating to the creation of Adam and Eve and their expulsion from the Garden of Eden, a unique example of a Genesis cycle in a church of this period.

All these scenes are painted in a severe, hieratic style, similar to that of the reliefs which cover the façades. Episodic details, indications of landscape or architecture are eliminated, when-ever they are not essential to an understanding of the scene portrayed. The figures stand motionless in a frontal or three-quarter view; the groups are shown in inverted perspective, the rows of heads lined one above the other; the folds of the draperies are reduced to geometric patterns which flatten the human form instead of revealing the shape of the limbs they cover. The artist also avoids portraying the emotions, even in such compositions as the Crucifixion, yet by their severe dignity and their monumental quality these paintings, despite their awkwardness, are strangely impressive.

This style characterizes the miniature painting of the tenth century. At times the decorative, abstract qualities were carried to extremes, as in the illustrated Gospel of 966, now in the Walters Art Galley. The seated Virgin and Child, and the standing evangelists, are puppet-like figures outlined against the neutral background of the parchment; the draperies, covered either with parallel or diagonal bands, or with a checker-board design in different colours, have hardly any connection with actual costumes, the painter's primary interest being in decorative patterns and in colour. At other times, and in the work of more skilled painters, the stylization was checked by a regard for the natural appearance of the human form. The Etchmiadzin Gospel, illustrated in 989, is the best example of this type: in the representations of the Virgin and Child, Christ enthroned between two apostles, and the standing evangelists, the figures are all two-dimensional, but the drapery folds follow in general the contours of the limbs. We see, in substance, a simplification rather than a transformation of a classical model, along the same lines as the paintings in the church at Aght'amar. In the manuscript, as well as in the wall paintings, the figures are shown frontally and all movement is eliminated, even in a scene like the Sacrifice of Isaac. In contradistinction to the figural miniatures, the arcades of the canon tables are solid constructions, recalling the architectural examples, with arches shown in relief and resting on heavy columns.

Plate 49

The few surviving examples of the tenth century do not provide a sufficiently wide view of the art of this period, and it is therefore difficult to decide whether or not the remains of the very fine wall paintings of the monastery of Tat'ev were executed in 930 by foreign painters, as reported in 1300 by the historian Stephen Orbelian. The large scene of the Last Judgment, with the dead rising from their tombs, is a most unusual composition and both this and the fragmentary Nativity differ in style from any known work in Armenia.

During the height of Bagratid power in the eleventh century, the kings, princes and high dignitaries of the realm commissioned luxury copies; this was also the period of Byzantine expansion, and Byzantine influence is much stronger in these paintings than in those of the preceding century. Some of the large miniatures of the Gospel of the Mekhitharist Library in Venice, known as the Trebizond Gospel because it was brought from that city to Venice, may in fact be the work of a Greek painter. The

Baptism, for example, compares most favourably with the best
Byzantine works; the figures, in particular John the Baptist and
Christ, are fully modelled and stand in natural, graceful poses;
in other compositions such as the Transfiguration a less plastic   Plate 51
treatment of the body, a slight stiffening of the attitudes betray
the hand of an Armenian artist. The canon tables have a wealth   Plate 54
of ornamental details of birds and plants, painted in rich colours
in which the blues predominate, and gold is lavishly used. If
this manuscript was, as seems probable, partly illustrated by a
Greek, the Gospel which King Gagik of Kars commissioned
was entirely the work of an Armenian who, while drawing his
inspiration from a Byzantine model, translated the style into his
own idiom and introduced many ornamental elements which
never appear in Byzantine manuscripts. These take the form of
vignettes painted in the margins. A host of birds forms a lively
border; they are sometimes perched on the initials, at other times
they are confronted, they frolic with one another or again are
shown in flight. The different species can often be recognized,   *Fig. 39*
though the forms are stylized, but the artist has also invented
imaginary creatures, constantly creating new combinations.
Other marginal ornaments imitate small rugs or textiles with
inscriptions simulating Cufic writing.

While in the usual type of Armenian Gospel manuscript
large full-page representations of the principal scenes of the life
of Christ are grouped together at the beginning, in the Gagik
Gospel miniatures have been introduced into the text. These
illustrated the Gospel narrative in great detail but a ruthless
hand has removed them and left only a few which allow us to
see the delicate style of these paintings. The most important
among the surviving miniatures is the group portrait of the king,
the queen and their daughter seated cross-legged on a low couch.   Plate 55
The king's tunic, Oriental in style, is made of a silk material
into which have been woven animals in roundels, the Sasanian
type of ornament that continued to be imitated in later centuries.

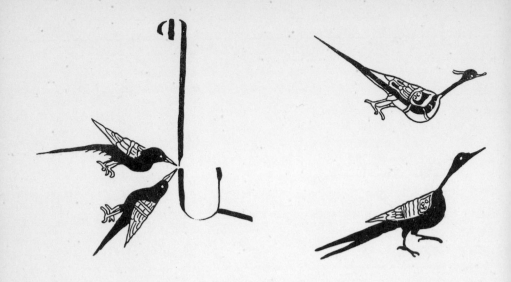

A similar design, with elephants and birds in roundels, decorates the cover of the couch.

Special mention should also be made of another sumptuous manuscript of this period, for it reveals a somewhat different aspect of the work done for wealthy patrons and helps us to see the variety of types and styles within this general group. This is the Gospel of the *Matenadaran* at Erevan, known as the Gospel of Moghni. In it, the early representations can still be recognized, but they are entirely transformed. Thus a Nilotic scene decorates the lunette of one of the canon tables, as in the Mlk'ē Gospel, but only one crocodile remains, the others have been replaced by griffins or human-headed quadrupeds; the sea has been eliminated and the composition entirely fills the lunette. The architectural setting of several Gospel scenes is ultimately derived from the type of Pompeian setting used in some Early Christian monuments and to which also belonged the background of the Adoration of the Magi in the sixth–seventh century Armenian miniature, but here the transformation is even more pronounced. Finally in the Gospel scenes, though the compositions agree, in

Plate 57

Plate 50

Fig. 39 Marginal miniatures in the Gospel of King Gagik of Kars (after Tchobanian)

the main, with Byzantine iconography, the transformation towards a linear style is more marked than in the preceding two manuscripts. The faces, specially those of the women, frequently recall the Armenian types. Thus these three manuscripts, though contemporary, present three stages of the departure from the Byzantine towards a national style.

This national style was better preserved in manuscripts which, unlike the luxury copies illustrated for members of the court circles, where the prestige of the imperial city was great, were produced in outlying or more conservative monasteries. The gold backgrounds and rich ornaments are absent from these manuscripts, the range of colours is limited as is also the number of figures in each scene. Many of the manuscripts of this series have been illustrated by men of little skill, but when produced by abler men these paintings appeal through the abstract qualities of the design and the expression of restrained emotion conveyed by the figures.

Plate 56

When, after a period of interruption caused by the Seljuk invasion, work is again resumed in the thirteenth and fourteenth

*Figs. 40–42 Gospel of Haghbat, dating from 1211. Portraits painted beside a canon table:
the binder of the manuscript; a servant of the monastery (the accompanying inscription reads: 'Sherenik,
bring fish whenever you come'); the Abbot of the monastery (after Durnovo)*

centuries the close contact with Byzantine models, revealed by
some of the luxury manuscripts, no longer exists. A more
familiar note appears in some of the illustrations where the
secondary figures of the Gospel scenes are sometimes attired in
contemporary costume; portraits of laymen and clerics appear
not simply as donors, but as an integral part of the illuminations.

Figs. 40–44   We see them, for instance, standing next to the canon tables;
one layman carries a jug of water, another a large fish; while on
another page of the same manuscript a young man is seated under
a tree, singing and playing a musical instrument. This secular
vein was to be further developed in the popular style of the
painters of the province of Vaspurakan.

Figs. 43, 44   Gospel of Haghbat. Portraits painted beside a canon table: a musician and a servant of the monastery (after Durnovo)

The products of this period show a considerable variety and there existed active scriptoria in large cities such as Erzinjan and Theodosiopolis as well as in the monastic schools, in particular that of the monastery of Gladzor. In the ornamental repertory, the geometric motifs of intricate interlaces take precedence over the floral ones which consist primarily of various forms of the palmette; birds continue to be represented in the margins but they are more highly stylized and they are often combined with floral interlaces.

Plate 58

Figs. 45, 46

The iconography of the Gospel scenes grouped at the beginning of the manuscript, conforms to the traditional types, but new scenes also appear, for instance in a Bible illustrated at Erzinjan,

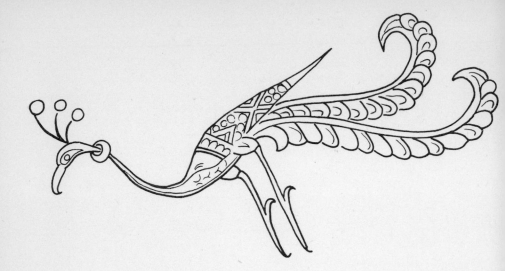

Plate 60

where the Vision of Ezekiel is an impressive and highly original composition.

Monumental painting also received a great impetus during this period. This may be partly due to Georgian influence and in the largest extant ensemble, the paintings of the church of St Gregory erected in 1215 by Tigran Honents', the inscriptions are in Georgian. The method of decoration follows, in the main, that used in Byzantine churches; the Ascension fills the dome, with a row of prophets below; Christ enthroned appears in the apse and the Communion of the Apostles is represented on the semicircular wall. The scenes from the life of Christ and the Virgin are depicted in the south and north zones of the

Plate 61

church while the west zone is given over to a detailed cycle of the life of St Gregory the Illuminator. Other churches at Ani

Plate 62

were also decorated with frescoes, of which there remain only fragments, and in these the Armenian style is more clearly marked. Portraits of donors were painted in some churches, for example at Haghbat and in the rock-cut church of the Virgin at Geghard, where the donor was represented with other members of his family.

Figs. 45, 46 Marginal ornaments of a manuscript illuminated at Mush in 1204. Erevan, Matenadaran, *no. 7729 (after Durnovo)*

In the kingdom of Cilicia, miniature painting attained a high degree of excellence. The ornamental pages of the manuscripts of the twelfth and thirteenth centuries are distinguished by the richness of their colouring, enhanced by the glittering gold background and by the great range of motives. The Armenian ornamental repertory is more varied than that of the Byzantine manuscript; at the same time the compositions avoid the heavy profusion of Muslim decoration. Birds run in and out of the floral scrolls of vine, acanthus or palmette, they are perched on the trees drawn at the sides of the canon tables; contorted or linked with one another they often form the initials of the Gospel lessons. Floral and geometric interlaces are constantly renewed in combinations where the fantasy of the artist is tempered by the logic and clarity of the composition. Imaginary creatures such as goat-headed men, nude women with long flowing hair, or nude men riding lions appear in the decoration of the canon tables; human and animal heads as well as birds replace the leaves of the floral scrolls and we see the curious situation in one manuscript of an animal composed of nude figures and also other animals.

Plate 63

Fig. 47
Plate 64

Plate 65

149

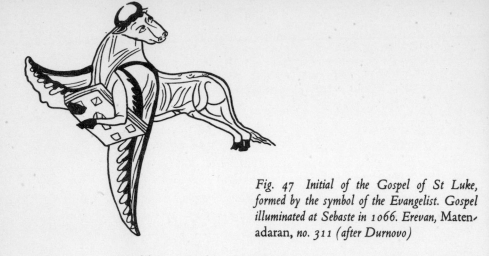

Plate 66

Plate 69

Plate 68

A like originality characterizes the extensive narrative cycle of the Gospel illustration, especially in the works of T'oros Roslin, the foremost painter of the thirteenth century who headed the scriptorium of the patriarchal see at Hromkla. The stateliness of the earlier compositions of the twelfth century has given place to a new spontaneity, to lively movement and life-like expressions which fit in with the familiar, narrative strain evinced by the iconography. T'oros Roslin frequently sets aside the time-honoured formulas, and interprets the Gospel story in a fresh manner. The intrusion of elements of daily life appears not only in the contemporary costumes occasionally worn by the secondary figures, as was the case in some manuscripts of Great Armenia, but in the actual compositions themselves; for instance, the Jews paying the thirty pieces of silver to Judas are represented like old merchants in a bazaar, weighing the silver on their scales, or the Magi returning home are accompanied by soldiers riding with banners flying, like the knights who accompanied the king on one of his expeditions. Without entirely breaking away from the past, T'oros Roslin thus frequently modifies the traditional themes, adding new ones which give a more vivid character to the narrative. His work shows a marked desire to express the delicate, tender feelings through graceful figures and harmonious compositions, but in the representations of the Passion cycle he also knows how to convey deeper emotions without exaggeration. The rigidity and stylization of the earlier period have been replaced by a more naturalistic treatment; the delicate shading and the arrangement of the folds of the draperies show the desire to reveal the rounded forms of the human figure. Men and women stand in graceful attitudes or briskly advance; the compositions are well ordered, avoiding whenever possible absolute symmetry. Certain elements in his work suggest that T'oros Roslin may have seen Western illuminated manuscripts. Acquaintance with such works of art no doubt broadened his horizon and may have developed his own natural tendencies, but the means by which this sensitive and imaginative artist enriched and revitalized the centuries-old tradition of Christian imagery are entirely his own.

Plate 67

Fig. 48 Shepherd of the Annunciation. Gospel illuminated by T'oros of Taron in 1307. Hartford Seminary, no. 3

A school of painters, active in the third quarter of the thirteenth century, gave a different impulse to Cilician painting. Among dated manuscripts this new style first appears in the beautiful illustrated Gospel produced in 1272 for Queen Keran, wife of Leo II (III) (Jerusalem no. 2563), and it develops in several other manuscripts, many of which are kept at the *Matenadaran* in Erevan. Movement is emphasized even in scenes which involve no definite action and an intense feeling is conveyed through the expression and attitudes of the principal figures, as well as through the participation of the secondary ones. Emotion is no longer restrained: in the Crucifixion the angels fly down in an agony of grief, Christ's body is sagging on the cross, and the Virgin, swooning under the weight of her sorrow, has to be supported by her companions. The scenery itself contributes to the dramatic effect of the compositions. In such scenes as the Transfiguration or the Raising of Lazarus, the rocky peaks of the mountains, twisted as it were by a supernatural force, enhance the awe-inspiring character of the event that is being portrayed. The pictorial technique, with the extensive use of gold high-lights and sudden colour changes in different areas of the draperies, differentiate these paintings from those of T'oros Roslin and his assistants. Finally, the repertory of ornamental effects is more extensive, and imaginary beings are more frequently represented.

Many Cilician manuscripts were commissioned by members of the royal family and their images as donors constitute an interesting portrait gallery. They vary considerably in composition. Prince Leo and his young wife Keran are represented dressed in the ceremonial Byzantine attire, and they are being blessed by Christ, while in the Gospel of 1272 written after their coronation the entire family is kneeling and small crowns, symbols of divine protection, descend in rays of light issuing

Plate 75

Plate 71

Plate 76

Fig. 49   Initial E from the Gospel illuminated by T'oros of Taron

Fig. 50　The horses of the Magi. Detail of the Nativity from a Gospel
in the style of Khizan, dating from 1332. Erevan, Matenadaran, no.
9423 (after Durnovo)

from Christ enthroned between the Virgin and John the Baptist. Plates 74, 77
At other times the kneeling donor is introduced to Christ by
the Virgin who spreads her mantle over the donor as a sign of her Plate 78
protection; or a bishop acts as an intercessor in presenting the
kneeling figure to the Virgin and Child. In the frontispiece of
the Assizes of Antioch, a judge pleads on behalf of a man kneeling
before the royal throne. In the Gospel illustrated for Bishop John,
the brother of King Het'um I, the donor is shown performing the Plate 72
functions of his office, that of ordaining deacons or priests.

The elegant style of the Cilician painters may still be seen in Plate 70
a few manuscripts of the early years of the fourteenth century.
The prolific painter Sargis Pitsak enjoyed a great reputation in Plate 73
his time, but his work, though technically skilled, lacks the
originality and vitality of the miniatures of the preceding century.

With the Mameluk conquest all artistic activity came to an
end in Cilicia, but it continued in Great Armenia well into the
seventeenth century. Cilician influence had spread in that
region; it was especially active in the important scriptoria such
as that of the monastery of Gladzor. The manuscripts illustrated

Figs. 48, 49

by the leading painter T'oros of Taron show on the one hand the survival of the style and iconography of the works produced in Great Armenia during the preceding century, and on the other the influence of Cilician painting, especially in the orna-mental compositions. Cilician influence is stronger in the

Plate 59

miniatures painted by Avag, whose work deserves to be better known. Regional schools also developed during this period, in particular in the area around Lake Van where different trends may be observed. The most interesting are the manuscripts illustrated at Khizan in a popular style that bears a strong

Fig. 50

oriental stamp.

Until fairly recently many of the published manuscripts belonged to the late centuries and happened to be mediocre works. But closer acquaintance with those which were illus-trated in Great Armenia during the ninth–eleventh centuries and in Cilicia in the twelfth–thirteenth centuries is bringing increasing recognition of the high quality of Armenian miniature painting and its place in the general history of medieval illumination.

Bibliography

CHAPTER I

ADONTZ, N. *Histoire d'Arménie. Les origines du Xe siècle au VIe av.J.C.* Paris, 1946.

AKURGAL, E. Urartäische Kunst, in *Anatolia*, IV. Ankara, 1959, pp. 77–114.

BARNETT, R. D. The excavations of the British Museum at Toprak Kale, near Van, in *Iraq*, XII, 1, 1950, pp. 1–43 and XVI, 1, 1954, pp. 3–22.

LEHMANN-HAUPT, C. F. *Armenien einst und jetzt*, I-II.2. Berlin, 1910–1931.

MARR, N. and SMIRNOV, J. *Les Vichaps.* Leningrad, 1931.

MELLINK, M. J. Anatolia: Old and New Perspectives, in *Proceedings of the American Philosophical Society*, 110.2, 1966.

OGANESIAN, K. L. *Karmir Blur IV. The architecture of Teishebaini* (in Russian). Erevan, 1955.

ÖZGÜÇ, T. The Urartian Architecture on the Summit of Altintepe, in *Anatolia*, VII, 1963, pp. 43–49.

PIOTROVSKII, B. B. *The history and civilization of Urartu* (in Russian). Erevan, 1944.

— *Karmir Blur I–III* (in Russian). Erevan, 1950–1955.

— *The Kingdom of Van (Urartu)* (in Russian). Moscow, 1959.

— *Urartu. The Kingdom of Van and its Art.* Translated from the Russian and ed. by Peter S. Gelling. London and New York, 1967.

SARDARIAN, S. H. *Primitive Society in Armenia* (in Armenian with English summary). Erevan, 1967.

TREVER, K. V. *Essays on the History and Culture of Ancient Armenia* (in Russian). Moscow, 1953.

CHAPTER II

ADONTZ, N. *Armenia at the time of Justinian* (in Russian). St Petersburg, 1908.

ASLAN, K. *Etudes historiques sur le peuple arménien.* Paris, 1928.

CHARANIS, P. *The Armenians in the Byzantine Empire* (Calouste Gulbenkian Foundation Armenian Library). Lisbon, 1964.

DER NERSESSIAN, S. *Armenia and the Byzantine Empire.* Cambridge (Mass.), 1947.

— Between East and West: Armenia and its divided history, in *The Dark Ages,* ed. by D. Talbot Rice. London, 1965, pp. 63–82.

EREMIAN, S. T. Principal features of the social regime of Armenia during the Hellenistic period (in Russian), in *Izvestija of the Armenian Academy of Sciences,* no. 11. Erevan, 1948.

GROUSSET, R. *Histoire de l'Arménie des origines à 1071.* Paris, 1947.

KURKDJIAN, V. M. *History of Armenia.* New York, 1962.

LAURENT, J. *L'Arménie entre Byzance et l'Islam depuis la conquête arabe jusqu'en 886.* Paris, 1919.

LYNCH, H. *Armenia : Travels and Studies,* 2 vols. London, 1901, and Connecticut, 1965.

MANANDIAN, H. *Critical Survey of the History of the Armenian people* (in Armenian), 4 vols. Erevan, 1945–1952.

— *Tigrane II et Rome.* Translated from the Armenian by H. Thorossian (Calouste Gulbenkian Foundation Armenian Library). Lisbon, 1963.

MORGAN, J. DE. *Histoire du peuple arménien.* Paris, 1919.

TIRATS'IAN, G. The Ervandunis in Armenia (in Armenian), in *Izvestija of the Armenian Academy of Sciences,* no. 6. Erevan, 1958.

TOUMANOFF, C. Armenia and Georgia, in *The Cambridge Medieval History,* vol. IV, ch. XIV. Cambridge, 1966.

— *Studies in Christian Caucasian History.* Georgetown University Press. Washington, D.C., 1963.

TOURNEBISE, F. *Histoire politique et religieuse de l'Arménie.* Paris, 1910.

CHAPTER III

ALISHAN, L. *Sissouan ou l'Arméno-Cilicie.* Venice, 1899.

— *Léon le Magnifique, premier roi de Sissouan ou de l'Arméno-Cilicie.* Venice, 1888.

CAHEN, CL. *La Syrie du Nord à l'époque des Croisades et la principauté franque d'Antioche.* Paris, 1940.

CANARD, M. Le royaume d'Arménie-Cilicie et les Mamelouks jusqu'au traité de 1285 in *Revue des Etudes Arméniennes*, N.S.IV, 1967, pp. 217–59.

DER NERSESSIAN, S. The Armenian Chronicle of the Constable Smpad or of the 'Royal Historian', in *Dumbarton Oaks Papers XIII*, 1959, pp. 143–68.

— The Kingdom of Cilician Armenia in K. H. Setton, *A History of the Crusades*, vol. II, pp. 630–59. Philadelphia, 1962.

DULAURIER, E. *Etude sur l'organisation politique, religieuse et administrative du royaume de la Petite-Arménie*. Paris, 1861.

GROUSSET, R. *Histoire des Croisades*. 3 vols. Paris, 1931–1936.

— *L'Empire du Levant*. Paris, 1949.

IORGA, N. *Brève histoire de la Petite Arménie*. Paris, 1930.

MIK'AELIAN, G. G. *History of the Armenian Cilician Kingdom* (in Russian). Erevan, 1952.

RÜDT-COLLENBERG, W. H. *The Rupenides, Hethumides and Lusignans. The structure of the Armeno–Cilician dynasties* (Calouste Gulbenkian Foundation Armenian Library). Paris, 1963.

RUNCIMAN, S. *A History of the Crusades*. 3 vols. Cambridge, 1953–1955, and New York, 1957, 1958.

CHAPTER IV

ALISHAN, L. *Assises d'Antioche reproduites en français et publiées au sixième centenaire de la mort de Sempad le Connétable*. Venice, 1876.

ARAK'ELIAN, B. *The cities and trades in Armenia in the IXth–XIIIth centuries* (in Armenian). Erevan, 1958.

BEDOUKIAN, P. Z. *Coinage of Cilician Armenia* (American Numismatic Society Numismatic Notes and Monographs, no. 147). New York, 1962.

DESIMONI, C. Actes passés en 1271, 1274 et 1279 à l'Aïas (Petite Arménie) et à Beyrouth par devant des notaires génois, in *Archives de l'Orient Latin*, 1881, pp. 434–534.

HAKOBIAN, S. E. *History of the Armenian peasantry. Period of early feudalism* (in Armenian). Erevan, 1957.

HEYD, W. *Histoire du commerce du Levant au Moyen Age*. 2 vols. Leipzig, 1936.

KHERUMIAN, R. Esquisse d'une féodalité oubliée, in *Vostan*, I, 1948–49, pp. 7–56.

— *The trade and cities of Armenia in relation to ancient world trade*. Translated from the second revised edition by N. G. Garsoian (Calouste Gulbenkian Foundation Armenian Library). Lisbon, 1965.

LANGLOIS, V. *Le Trésor des chartes d'Arménie*. Paris, 1863.

MANANDIAN, H. A. *Feudalism in ancient Armenia* (in Armenian). Erevan, 1934.

SERJEANT, R. B. Material for a history of Islamic textiles up to the Mongol conquest, in *Ars Islamica*, X, 1943, pp. 91–100.

CHAPTER V

ARPEE, L. *A History of Armenian Christianity*. New York, 1946.

CARRIERE, A. *Les huit sanctuaires de l'Arménie payenne d'après Agathange et Moïse de Khoren*. Paris, 1899.

KARST, J. *Mythologie arméno-caucasienne et hétito-asianique*. Strasbourg–Zurich, 1948.

ORMANIAN, M. *Azgapatum. History of the Armenian nation* (in Armenian), 3 vols. Constantinople–Jerusalem, 1913–1927.

— *The church of Armenia*. Translated from the French by G. M. Gregory. Oxford, 1912, and Illinois, 1955.

SARKISSIAN, K. *The Council of Chalcedon and the Armenian Church*. London, 1965, and Illinois, 1965.

CHAPTER VI

ABEGHIAN, M. *History of ancient Armenian literature* (in Armenian), vol. I. Erevan, 1944.

BONFANTE, G. Armenians and Phrygians, in *Armenian Quarterly*, I, 1946, pp. 82–97.

BOYAJIAN, Z. C. *Armenian legends and poems*. London–New York, 1958, and New York, 1959.

DAVID OF SASSOUN: *The Armenian Folk Epic in Four Cycles*. Edited and translated by A. K. Shalian. Athens (Ohio), 1964.

DOWSETT, C. J. F. *The History of the Caucasian Albanians* by Movses Dasxuranci. London, 1961.

GARITTE, G. *Documents pour l'étude du livre d'Agathange*. Studi e testi, 127. Vatican City, 1946.

GREGOIRE DE NAREK, *Le livre de prières*. Introduction, traduction de l'arménien et notes par I. Kéchichian, S.J. Paris, 1961.

GREGORY OF AKNER, *History of the Nation of the Archers (the Mongols).* Edited with an English translation and notes by R. P. Blake and R. N. Frye. Cambridge (Mass.), 1954.

LANGLOIS, V. Mémoire sur la vie et les écrits du prince Grégoire Magistros, in *Journal asiatique*, I, 1869.

LEROY, M. Grégoire Magistros et les traductions arméniennes d'auteurs grecs, in *Annuaire de l'Institut de philologie et d'histoire orientale*. Brussels, III, 1935.

MEILLET, A. *Esquisse d'une grammaire comparée de l'Arménien classique.* Vienna, 1936.

PEETERS, P. Pour l'histoire des origines de l'alphabet arménien, in *Revue des Etudes Arméniennes*, IX, 1929, pp. 203–37.

TCHOBANIAN, A. *La Roseraie d'Arménie.* 3 vols. Paris, 1918–1929.

THOROSSIAN, H. *Histoire de la littérature arménienne des origines jusqu'à nos jours.* Paris, 1951. (All the translations of the Armenian historians published before 1951 are listed in this work.)

CHAPTER VII

Architettura medievale armena. Roma, Palazzo Venezia, 10–30 giugno 1968. Rome, 1968 (Catalogue with articles by G. de Francovich, F. de Maffei, H. Kh. Vahramian, T. B. Fratadocchi, P. Cuneo, E. Costa).

ARAK'ELIAN, B. *Garni. Results of the excavations* (in Armenian). Erevan, I–III, 1951, 1957, 1962.

BACHMANN, W. *Kirchen und Moscheen in Armenien und Kurdistan.* Leipzig, 1913.

BALTRUSAÏTIS, J. *Le problème de l'ogive et l'Arménie.* Paris, 1936.

BROSSET, M. F. *Les ruines d'Ani.* St Petersburg, 1861.

BUNIATIAN, N. G. *The pagan temple near the palace of Trdat at the fortress of Garni* (in Russian). Erevan, 1933.

CUNEO, P. La basilique de Tsitsernakavank dans Karabagh, in *Revue des Etudes Arméniennes*, N.S.IV, 1967, pp. 203–16.

EREMIAN, A. *The church of Ripsimé* (in Russian). Erevan, 1955.

GRABAR, A. *Martyrium. Recherches sur le culte des reliques et l'art chrétien antique.* 2 vols. Paris, 1946.

HARUTIUNIAN, V. M. and SAFARIAN, S. A. *Monuments of Armenian architecture* (in Russian). Moscow, 1951.

KAFADARIAN, K. *Haghbat. Architectural monuments and inscriptions* (in Armenian). Erevan, 1963.

— *The monastery of Sanahin and its inscriptions* (in Armenian). Erevan, 1957.

— *The town of Dvin and its excavations* (in Armenian). Erevan, 1952.

KHATCHATRIAN, A. *L'architecture arménienne*. Paris, 1949.

— Les églises cruciformes du Tayq, in *Cahiers Archéologiques*, XVII, 1967, pp. 203–208.

— Les monuments funéraires des IVe–VIIe siècles et leurs analogies syriennes, in *Byzantinische Forschungen*, I, 1966, pp. 179–92.

— A propos des niches extérieures dans l'architecture arménienne, in *Synthronon. Bibliothèque des Cahiers Archéologiques II*. Paris, 1968, pp. 69–73.

KRAUTHEIMER, R. *Early Christian and Byzantine Architecture*. Harmondsworth and New York, 1965.

MILLET, G. *L'école grecque dans l'architecture byzantine*. Paris, 1916.

MNATSAKANIAN, S. Kh. *The architecture of the Armenian ante-chapels* (in Russian). Erevan, 1952.

— *The school of Siunik' of Armenian architecture* (in Armenian). Erevan, 1960.

SAHINIAN, A. *The architecture of the basilica of K'asakh* (in Armenian with Russian summary). Erevan, 1955.

— Recherches scientifiques sous les voûtes de la cathédrale d'Etchmiadzine, in *Revue des Etudes Arméniennes*, N.S.III, 1966, pp. 41–71.

STRZYGOWSKI, J. *Die Baukunst der Armenier und Europa*, 2 vols. Vienna, 1918.

TCHUBINASHVILI, G. P. *Researches in Armenian architecture* (in Russian with German summary). Tbilisi, 1967.

THIERRY, J. M. Monastères arméniens du Vaspurakan, in *Revue des Etudes Arméniennes*, N.S.IV, 1967, pp. 167–86.

THIERRY, N. and M. Notes sur des monuments arméniens en Turquie (1964), in *Revue des Etudes Arméniennes*, N.S.II, 1965, pp. 165–84.

THORAMANIAN, Th. *Materials for the history of Armenian architecture* (in Armenian), 2 vols. Erevan, 1942, 1948.

TOKARSKI, N. M. *The architecture of Armenia. IVth–XIVth centuries* (in Russian). Erevan, 1961.

CHAPTER VIII

ARAK'ELIAN, B. *Armenian figurative sculpture from the IVth to the VIIth century* (in Armenian). Erevan, 1949.

BALTRUSAÏTIS, J. *Etudes sur l'art médiéval en Géorgie et en Arménie*. Paris, 1929.

BEDOUKIAN, P. Z. A classification of the coins of the Artaxiad dynasty of Armenia, in *The American Numismatic Society. Museum Notes* 14, 1968.

DER NERSESSIAN, S. *Aght'amar. Church of the Holy Cross*. Cambridge (Mass.), 1965.

— Le reliquaire de Skevra et l'orfèvrerie cilicienne aux XIIIe et XIVe siècles, in *Revue des Etudes Arméniennes*, N.S.I, 1964, pp. 121–47.

HOVSEP'IAN, G. *Materials and studies on the history of Armenian art and culture* (in Armenian with English summary), vol. II. New York, 1944.

IPŞIROĞLU, M. S. *Die Kirche von Achtamar. Bauplastik im Leben des Lichtes*. Berlin und Mainz, 1963.

IZMAILOVA, T. and AIVAZIAN, M. *Armenian art* (in Russian). Moscow, 1962.

SAKISIAN, A. *Pages d'art arménien*. Paris, 1940.

SEYRIG, H. Trésor monétaire de Nisibe, in *Revue numismatique*, 1955, pp. 85–128.

CHAPTER IX

ARAK'ELIAN, R. The newly discovered mosaic of Garni (in Russian), in *Izvestija of the Armenian Academy of Sciences*, no. 7, pp. 111–18. Erevan, 1954.

AZARIAN, L. *Cilician miniature painting* (in Armenian). Erevan, 1964.

BANATEANU, Gl. La fresque en Arménie à l'époque ancienne et au Moyen Age, in *Studia et Acta Orientalia*, I, 1957, pp. 49–63.

— Ein vernachlässigter Zweig der armenischen Kunst: die Mosaik, in *Bysantinoslavica*, XIX, 1958, pp. 107–18.

DER NERSESSIAN, S. *Armenian Manuscripts in the Freer Gallery of Art*. Smithsonian Institution. Freer Gallery of Art. Oriental Studies, no. 6. Washington D.C., 1963.

— *The Chester Beatty Library. Catalogue of the Armenian Manuscripts with an Introduction on the History of Armenian Art.* 2 vols. Dublin, 1958.

— The Date of the Initial Miniatures of the Etchmiadzin Gospel, in *The Art Bulletin*, 15, 1933, pp. 327–60.

— Un Evangile cilicien du XIIIe siècle, in *Revue des Etudes Arméniennes*, N.S.IV, 1967, pp. 103–19.

— *Manuscrits arméniens illustrés des 12e, 13e, et 14e siècles de la Bibliothèque des Pères Mekhitharistes de Venise*, 2 vols. Paris, 1937.

— La peinture arménienne au VIIe siècle et les miniatures de l'évangile d'Etchmiadzin, in *Actes du XIIe Congrès International des Etudes Byzantines*. Belgrade, 1964, vol. III, pp. 49–57.

DJANACHIAN, M. *Armenian miniatures at the monastic Library of S. Lazzaro.* Venice, 1964.

DURNOVO, L. A. *Brief history of ancient Armenian painting* (in Russian). Erevan, 1957.

— *Miniatures Arméniennes*. Paris, 1960.

DURNOVO L. A. and DRAMPIAN, R. *Armenian Miniatures* (in Armenian, Russian and French). Erevan, 1967.

GRABAR, A. Etudes sur la tradition arménienne dans l'art médiéval, in *Revue des Etudes Arméniennes*, N.S.III, 1966, pp. 31–37.

IZMAILOVA, T. A. The artistic decoration of the Armenian manuscript of the year 1053 (in Russian), in *Vestnik Matenadarana*, 5, 1960, pp. 239–76.

— L'Iconographie du cycle des fêtes d'un groupe de codex arméniens d'Asie Mineure, in *Revue des Etudes Arméniennes*, N.S.IV, 1967, pp. 125–66.

— L'Iconographie du manuscrit du Matenadaran no. 2877, in *Revue des Etudes Arméniennes*, N.S. I, 1964, pp. 149–87, and II, 1965, pp. 185–222.

— Tables des Canons de deux manuscrits arméniens d'Asie Mineure du XIe siècle, in *Revue des Etudes Arméniennes*, N.S. III, 1966, pp. 91–117.

MACLER, F. *L'Enluminure arménienne profane.* Paris, 1928.

STRZYGOWSKI, J. *Das Etchmiadzin-Evangeliar.* Byzantinische Denkmäler II. Vienna, 1891.

— *Kleinarmenische Miniaturmalerei. Die Miniaturen des Tübingen Evangeliars MA. XIII. 1.* Tübingen, 1907.

SVIRIN, A. N. *Miniature painting in ancient Armenia* (in Russian). Moscow-Leningrad, 1939.

WEITZMANN, K. *Die armenische Buchmalerei des 10. und beginnenden 11. Jahrhunderts.* Istanbuler Forschungen, 4. Bamberg, 1933.

Sources of Illustrations

Grateful acknowledgment is made by the author to the following persons and institutions for many of the photographs used in the plates: Mr. L. Azarian and the Historical Museum of Erevan, 3, 4, 8, 22, 23, 25–29, 38, 42, 47; Mr. P. Bedoukian, 6; Mrs. N. Thierry, 9–12, 14, 20, 21, 30–33, 40; the Ecole des Hautes Etudes, Paris, 13, 15, 19, 39, 51–54, 63; Professor D. Lang, 17; the Cabinet des Medailles at the Bibliothèque Nationale, Paris, 24; Mr. J. Donat, 34, 35; the Hermitage Museum, Leningrad, 43, 44, 62; the *Matenadaran*, Erevan, 49, 56–58, 66; Editions Cercle d'Art, Paris, 50; Mr. P. Cuneo, 61; the Walters Art Gallery, Baltimore, 64, 67; Mrs. T. Izmailova, 65, 71, 72; the Freer Gallery of Art, Washington, 69; the Library of Congress, Washington, 74–77.

Figs. 2–5, 8, 10–17, 19, 21–28, 30, 31, 33–50 were drawn by Miss Gillian Jones, and Fig. 7 by S. Schotten.

1

2

3

4

5

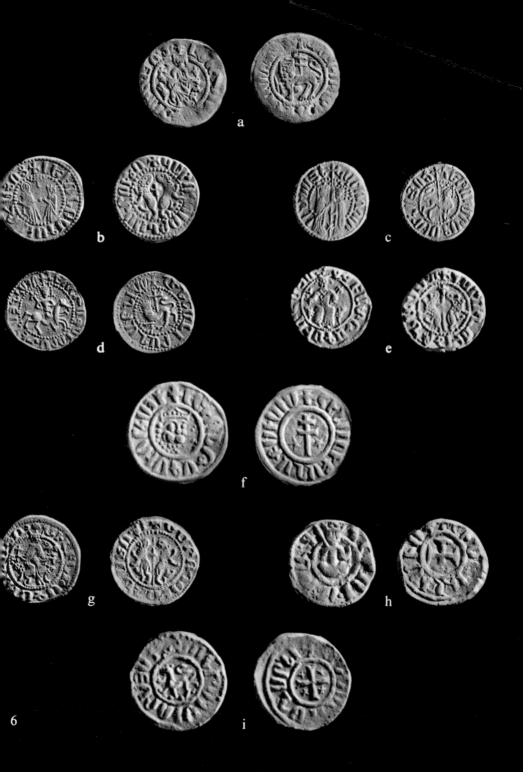

6

8

9

13

14

15

16

17

8

19

20

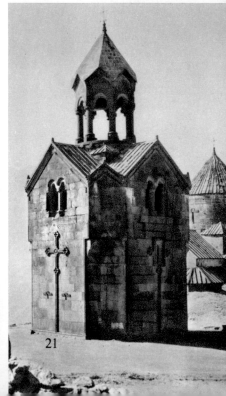

21

22

24

25

26

23

27   28

29

30

31

32

33

34

35

36

37

38

39

40

41

42

43

44

45

46

47

48, 49

50

51

52

53

4

55

56

57, 58

59

60

61

62

64

65

66

67

68

69

70   72

71 73

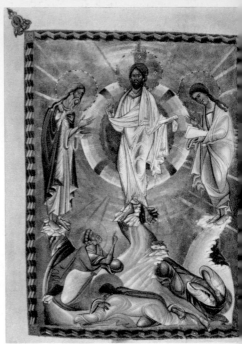

75

76

77

78

Notes on the Plates

1 View of Mount Ararat.

2 Fortifications of Ani.

3 Urartian bronze statuette, probably representing the goddess Arubani, the consort of Haldi. The pendant on her breast is shaped like a dagger, topped by a recumbent lion. Height: 12 cm. Erevan, Armenian Historical Museum.

4 Small gold bowl of the Early Bronze Age decorated with pairs of confronted lions. Found at Kirovakan. Erevan, Armenian Historical Museum.

5 Head of a bronze statue of Aphrodite found at Erzinjan. In Antiquity the city was called Erez and the most important shrine of the goddess had been erected there. London, British Museum.

6 Cilician coins. Actual size. New York, Paul Bedoukian Collection.
(a) Gold coin of Leo I (1198–1219). *Obv.* King enthroned, full-face, holding a cross in his right, and a fleur-de-lys in his left hand. *Rev.* Lion, facing left, holding a cross.

(b) Coronation drachm of Leo I (1198–1219). *Obv.* Christ standing, and opposite him the King, crowned and kneeling. *Rev.* Two lions, rampant, regardant, with a cross between them.

(c) Silver drachm of Het'um I and Zabel (1226–1270). *Obv.* The King and Queen crowned, facing each other and together holding a cross. *Rev.* Lion, facing right, holding a cross.

(d) Silver drachm of Leo II (1270–1289). *Obv.* King crowned, on horseback, facing right and holding a sceptre. *Rev.* Lion, facing right, holding a cross.

(e) Silver drachm of Smbat (1296–1298). *Obv.* King enthroned, full-face. *Rev.* Two lions rampant, regardant, with a cross between them.

(f) Copper coin of Leo I (1198–1219). *Obv.* Leonine head of the King, crowned. *Rev.* Tall cross with two stars at the sides.

(g) Coronation drachm of Oshin (1308–1320). *Obv.* King enthroned, full-face, holding cross and fleur-de-lys. *Rev.* Two lions rampant, regardant, with a cross between them.

(h) Copper coin of Het'um II (1289–1307). *Obv.* King seated cross-legged in Oriental fashion, full-face, and holding a sceptre in his right hand. *Rev.* Simple cross.

(i) Copper coin of Leo II (1270–89). *Obv.* Lion walking left. *Rev.* Cross with four stars.

7 Fragment of a silk fabric inside the binding of an Armenian manuscript written between 1187 and 1212. The large roundels enclose confronted birds on either side of a conventionalized tree; the border of the roundel, edged with pearls, is decorated with four pairs of confronted peacocks at the sides of heart-shaped motifs placed in the diagonal axes. The curvilinear lozenges between the roundels are decorated with eight pine cones placed in a circle around a disc edged with pearls and enclosing a rosette formed by four heart-shaped leaves. Ninth–tenth century. Erevan, Matenadaran, No. 6263.

8 Ruins of the peripteral temple of Garni, built in the first century AD and restored in the third century. Entrance view, with nine steps leading to the pronaos. The bases and lower sections of some of the columns can be seen.

9 Church at Mren, built in 639–640. View of the dome with the octagonal drum resting on squinches.

10 T'alin. Cathedral. Seventh century. View from the north-east.

11 Ashtarak. Church known as Karmravor. Seventh century. View from the south-west.

12 Mastara. Cathedral of St John. Seventh century. View from the north-east.

13 Ani. Cathedral. The construction begun in 989 during the reign of Smbat II was completed in 1001 by Gagik I and Queen Katramide. Designed by the architect Trdat. View from the north-west.

14 Vagharshapat. Church of St Hrip'simē, built by the Catholicos Komitas in 618.

15 Ani. Church of the Redeemer, built in 1036. In recent years half of the building has collapsed.

16 Kars. Cathedral of the Holy Apostles. Tenth century. View from the north-west.

17 Aght'amar. Church of the Holy Cross, built by Gagik I Artsruni between 915 and 921. The porch in front of the south door is a later addition.

18 Marmashen. Cathedral, built between 986 and 1029. View from the north-west.

19 Ani. Ante-chapel *(zhamatun)* added in the twelfth century to the church of the Holy Apostles.

20 Amaghu-Noravank. Church of the Virgin built by Prince Burt'el in 1339. View after it had been restored. On the tympanum above the door of the lower storey, the Virgin and Child enthroned between the archangels Gabriel and Michael; on the tympanum of the upper storey, Christ between the apostles Peter and Paul.

21 Haghbat. Bell tower built by the abbot Hamazasp in 1245. On the right, the church of the Holy Sign, built between 976 and 991.

22 Garni. Fragments from the entablature of the temple.

23 Garni. Ionic capital from the temple.

24 Tetradrachm of Tigran the Great (95–56 BC). *Obv*. Portrait of the King wearing the Armenian tiara. *Rev*. Tyche of Antioch and inscription *Basileos Tigranou*. Diam. 2.8 cm. Paris, Bibliothèque Nationale, Cabinet des Médailles.

25 Upper part of a stele *(khatchk'ar)* from T'alin representing the Baptism. Above, an angel flying down with a crown; below, the dove descending on Christ with a jewelled crown in its beak. The lower part of the stele is destroyed. Seventh century. Height 1.20 m.

26 Rear view of the same stele. Above, an angel, holding the globe in his left hand and raising his right hand; below, a nimbed figure holding a cross-shaped staff.

27 Base of the stele from T'alin, measuring 76 by 86 cm. Front view: Virgin and Child enthroned between two angels.

28 Another stone stele from T'alin. Above, the saint holding a book probably represents St Gregory 'the Illuminator'. Below, King Trdat in the porcine aspect he had assumed before his conversion. Seventh century. Height 1.65 metres.

29 Fragment of a stone lintel found in the cemetery of the village of Upper Artashat, near Dvin. Vintage scene to one side of a central cross framed by ornate leaves. Sixth–seventh century. Size: 1.20 by 0.65 metres.

30 Church at Mren. Detail of the lintel over the west portal representing a saint and one of the donors, Nerseh Kamsarakan or David Saharuni. To the left of these two figures appear Christ between St Peter and St Paul, and on the extreme left, the other donor. Two angels in frontal view occupy the tympanum. The donor is clad in a fur coat with long sleeves hanging loosely at the sides.

31 Church of Zvart'nots'. Capital from one of the columns of the exedra (641–666). The wings of the eagle spread over the two sides of the capital.

32 Church of Zvart'nots'. Basket capital surmounted by Ionic volutes from one of the columns of the exedra. The monogram of Nerses, in Greek letters, is carved between the volutes. The other monogram in Greek, not visible on the photograph, spells the word Catholicos.

33 T'alin. Cathedral. Seventh century. Blind arcade of the north façade decorated with a pomegranate branch.

34 Aght'amar. Church of the Holy Cross (915–921). Upper half of the east façade. Running animals under the roof of the dome and under the eaves; beneath the gable, St John the Evangelist blessing and holding the Gospel. Below, vine scroll having at the centre the King holding a cup and plucking grapes, accompanied by two attendants. In the roundel, quarter-length figure of Adam.

35 Aght'amar. Church of the Holy Cross. Left end of the south façade. Episodes from the story of Jonah: Jonah cast into the sea; Jonah, ejected by the whale, sleeping under the gourd tree; Jonah addressing the King of Nineveh and the inhabitants of Nineveh represented in medallions. The medallion figures above the Jonah scenes represent Stephen the protomartyr, the prophets Zephaniah and Elijah. The third figure is not identified by an inscription.

36 Aght'amar. Church of the Holy Cross. West façade. King Gagik holding a model of the church. He is clad in a long tunic decorated with rows of concentric and interlocking circles. The design on his rich mantle consists of birds framed by interlocking circles and five-lobed leaves placed between the circles. The crown is partly broken, but one can still see a wing-like motif on the right, which is derived from Sasanian crowns.

37 Portrait of King Gagik I, now lost, which once adorned the church of St Gregory erected by him at Ani. In his outstretched hands the king bore a model of the church. Gagik is clothed in the Oriental costume of the time, a long coat with wide sleeves, with a large turban on his head.

38 Niche on the east façade of the church of the Holy Sign at Haghbat (built 991). The two brothers, Gurgen (Kiurike I) on the left and King Smbat II on the right, hold a model of the church. Smbat, as King of Ani, wears a large turban like the one worn later by Gagik I (*see* plate 37).

39 Stele from the monastery of Sanahin, twelfth–thirteenth century. The delicately carved ornaments stand out against the shadow of the back‑ground which has been cut away. A different combination of linear interlace is used in each one of the lateral compartments.

40 Haghbat. Stele erected by the abbot Hovhannes in 1273, as a memorial for himself and for the *amirspasalar* Sadun. In the upper register, an abbre‑viated representation of the Ascension. Below, Christ crucified with the donors at the foot of the cross, and the twelve apostles in the lateral rectangles.

41 Amaghu‑Noravank. Church of St John the Baptist. Detail of the tympanum carving dated 1321. The Virgin and Child enthroned; on the left, bust of a prophet and part of an inscription in the floral scroll.

42 Carved wooden gates, formerly part of the church of the Holy Apostles at Mush. Dated by the inscription to 1134. Rider saints and other riders are represented in the upper frame of the door, and animals running in a floral scroll on the two side frames. Erevan, Armenian Historical Museum.

43 Silver reliquary in the form of a triptych made in 1293 at the monastery of Skevra in Cilicia, by order of Bishop Constantine. The Crucifixion in the centre and the Annunciation on the wings. The medallion figures represent: centre, St Paul and St Peter; left, John the Baptist and David; right, Stephen the protomartyr and King Het'um II kneeling. Lenin‑grad, Hermitage Museum.

44 The same reliquary with the wings closed. Standing figures: St Gregory 'the Illuminator' and the apostle Thaddeus. Medallions: above, St Peter and St Paul; below, St Eustratius and St Vardan, the hero of the battle of Avarayr in the fifth century.

45 Silver binding made in 1254 at the patriarchal see of Hromkla. Christ enthroned surrounded by the symbols of the four Evangelists. The inscription on the quatrefoil gives the date and the name of the Bishop Step'anos who commissioned the binding. The manuscript itself, a Gospel, had been illustrated for the same bishop in 1248. Antilias (Lebanon) Catholicosate of Cilicia, MS. No. 1.

46 Part of the apse painting of the church of Lmbat (seventh century) representing the Vision of Ezekiel combined with the Vision of Isaiah. To the left, part of the aureole of Christ can be seen; next to it, the flaming wheel and a tetramorph whose wings are covered with eyes.

47 Bronze censer found at Ani (twelfth–thirteenth century). The scenes represented are as follows: The Nativity, the Adoration of the Magi, the Crucifixion, the Resurrection. Erevan, Armenian Historical Museum, No. 1316.

48 Ivory binding of the Etchmiadzin Gospel, sixth century. Front cover. In the centre, the Virgin and Child enthroned between angels; at the sides, scenes from the life of the Virgin and the Infancy of Christ; below, the Adoration of the Magi; above, cross in a wreath borne by flying angels. Erevan, *Matenadaran*, No. 2374.

49 Etchmiadzin Gospel, copied and illustrated in 989 at the monastery of Noravank' in the province of Siunik'. Virgin orans with the Child on her knees. The other figural representations grouped at the beginning of the manuscript represent: Christ between two saints; the four Evangelists and the Sacrifice of Abraham. Erevan, *Matenadaran*, No. 2374.

50 Etchmiadzin Gospel. The Adoration of the Magi, sixth–seventh century. This is one of two leaves bound at the end of the tenth-century manuscript. The other miniatures represent: the Annunciation to Zachariah; the Annunciation to the Virgin, and the Baptism. Erevan, *Matenadaran*, No. 2374.

51 Venice, San Lazzaro. Known as the Trebizond Gospel because it was brought from that city to Venice. Fol. 3, the Transfiguration. While

some of the miniatures were probably executed by a Greek painter, others, like the present scene, were the work of Armenians imitating a Byzantine model. Eleventh century. Mekhitharist Library, No. 1400.

52 Gospel of Queen Mlk'ē, illustrated in 862 and presented later by her to the monastery of Varag. Fol. 8, The Ascension of Christ. Christ and the Virgin are clothed in purple. The angels on either side of Christ wear the Byzantine imperial attire: a purple chlamys over a white tunic, and red shoes. Venice, San Lazzaro, Mekhitharist Library, No. 1144.

53 The same Gospel, Fol. 2. End of the Letter of Eusebius, framed by an archway with Nilotic scene in the tympanum.

54 Canon table from the Trebizond Gospel. Votice crowns hang from the lower band of the rectangle. The plant forms at the sides of the rect-angle and columns are a characteristic feature of the decoration of the canon tables in Armenian manuscripts.

55 Gospel of King Gagik of Kars, illustrated before 1064. Portrait of the King, the Queen and their daughter. The miniature is partly mutilated. The purple silk robe of Gagik is decorated with large roundels edged with pearls and each enclosing an ibex. Traces of Kufic letters can be seen on the *tiraz* bands of the sleeves. The design of the couch cover con-sists of large roundels enclosing saddled elephants and smaller roundels which frame birds or floral motifs. Jerusalem, Armenian Patriarchate, No. 2556.

56 Gospel dating from 1038. Fol. 5v, the Baptism of Christ. This manus-cript is one of the best examples of the 'abstract' tendencies of the artist, his emphasis on design and rhythm rather than on plastic form. Erevan, *Matenadaran*, No. 6201.

57 Gospel of Moghni, eleventh century. Fol. 18v, the Last Supper. The miniatures grouped at the beginning of the manuscript represent the principal events in the life of Christ. Erevan, *Matenadaran*, No. 7736.

58 Gospel of 'the Translators', illustrated in 1232 in Great Armenia. The artist's tendency to stylize all the forms is particularly noticeable in his treatment of the landscape. Erevan, *Matenadaran*, No. 2743.

59 Gospel illustrated *c.* 1334–1336 by the painter Avag. Fol. 5v, Entry of Christ into Jerusalem. The full-page miniatures grouped at the beginning of the manuscript represent the principal events in the life of Christ. In the British Museum Gospel, Or. 5304, illustrated by the same painter, the miniatures, introduced into the text, are more numerous but unfortunately the colours have flaked. Jerusalem, Armenian Patriarchate, No. 1941.

60 Bible written at Erzinjian in 1269 for Archbishop Sargis and his son Hovhannes by three scribes, Mkhit'ar, Hakovbos and Movses. Fol. 414v, Ezekiel's vision by the river Chebar. Below, Ezekiel is lying by the river and the angel presents to him the scroll that he was bidden to eat. Jerusalem, Armenian Patriarchate, No. 1925.

61 Painting from the church of St Gregory at Ani, erected by Tigran Honents' in 1215. Scene from the life of St Gregory 'the Illuminator'.

62 Painting from the destroyed church of Baghtaker at Ani, twelfth century. Head of the Virgin. Leningrad, Hermitage Museum.

63 Gospel illustrated in 1193 at the monastery of Skevra, in Cilicia, for Prince Het'um of Lambron and his brother Archbishop Nerses of Lambron by the scribe Kostandin. Fol. 2, end of the Letter of Eusebius to Carpianus. In the lunette, quarter-length figure of Carpianus. Venice, San Lazzaro, Mekhitharist Library, No. 1635.

64 Gospel illustrated in 1262 at Hromkla by T'oros Roslin, for the priest T'oros, nephew of the Catholicos Constantine I. Fol. 131, first page of the Gospel of St Mark. The first letter is formed by the lion, symbol of the evangelist. Baltimore, Walters Art Gallery, No. 539.

65 Cilician Gospel of the thirteenth century. Fol. 1v, canon table. In the triangular sections of the rectangle, nude figures are riding on lions.

Human-headed birds and quadrupeds, combined with floral motifs, fill the central section. Erevan, *Matenadaran*, No. 9422.

66 Book of Prayers of Nerses of Narek, illustrated in 1173 for Archbishop Nerses of Lambron by the scribe Grigor. Fol. 7v, portrait of Nerses of Narek, writing. Erevan, *Matenadaran*, No. 1568.

67 Gospel illustrated in 1262 at Hromkla by T'oros Roslin. Fol. 66, Angels ministering to Christ after the Temptation. Baltimore, Walters Art Gallery, No. 539.

68 Gospel illustrated in 1268 at Hromkla by T'oros Roslin, for the Catholicos Constantine. Fol. 182, the Nativity. Jerusalem, Armenian Patriarchate, No. 3627.

69 Gospel illustrated in Cilicia for Prince Vasak, thirteenth century. School of T'oros Roslin. P. 168, the Jews paying the thirty pieces of silver to Judas. Washington, Freer Gallery of Art, No. 32.18.

70 Gospel illustrated in 1316 at Tarsus by Levon Lazrts'i. Fol. 21v, portrait of St Matthew. Jerusalem, Armenian Patriarchate, No. 1950.

71 Gospel illustrated in 1287 for Archbishop John, brother of Het'um I. Fol. 101v, the Crucifixion. Erevan, *Matenadaran*, No. 197.

72 The same Gospel, Fol. 341v, Archbishop John ordaining a deacon. Erevan, *Matenadaran*, No. 197.

73 Hymnal illustrated in 1335 at Sis by Sargis Pitsak. Fol. 1v, Anna praying beside a tree with a nest of swallows, as mentioned in the apocryphal Gospel of the Infancy of Christ; behind her stands Joachim. This miniature accompanies the hymn on the Nativity of the Virgin. Jerusalem, Armenian Patriarchate, No. 1578.

74 Gospel illustrated in 1262 at Hromkla by T'oros Roslin. Fol. 288, portrait of Prince Leo and Princess Keran receiving Christ's benediction. Jerusalem, Armenian Patriarchate, No. 2660.

75 Gospel illustrated in Cilicia in 1272 for Queen Keran. Fol. 23, the Baptism of Christ. Jerusalem, Armenian Patriarchate, No. 2563.

76 Fol. 69 from the same manuscript, the Transfiguration.

77 Fol. 380 from the same manuscript, portraits of King Leo and Queen Keran and their children receiving Christ's benediction, enthroned between the Virgin and John the Baptist. The manuscript was illustrated in 1272, the year of their coronation.

78 Gospel illustrated for Prince Vasak, brother of King Het'um I. Second half of the thirteenth century. Vasak and his two sons presented to Christ by the Virgin. Jerusalem, Armenian Patriarchate, No. 2568.

Index

Index